The Journey to CEO Success

"Patrick nailed it! I LOVE the seven practices. They deliver the foundational steps for success in business. Arbill is living proof!"

— Julie Copeland, CEO and President, Arbill

"Patrick Thean's *The Journey to CEO Success* is a masterclass in leadership and growth. As a client of Patrick's during some of my company's most pivotal moments, I can attest that this book contains the key wisdom that helped me succeed as a CEO and will be an indispensable guide for any leader aiming to navigate the complexities of CEO life with grace and success."

— Mort O'Sullivan, Founder, ARCA

"Mike never focused on the risk that AvidXchange might not be successful, but always on creating a culture of winning. He knew growing his leadership skills and nurturing a culture of teamwork was core to building a great company."

— Jim Hausman, former public company CFO; Board Member, AvidXchange

"Having seen Mike grow his company from $30mm to $500mm in revenue, and even more importantly, grow enormously as a leader, I am grateful that he's taken the time to share his journey and insights with the world."

- Matthew Harris, Partner, Bain Capital

"Michael Praeger has a rare combination of operational strength and optimism that has powered AvidXchange to its current success with his great executive team. This book is a step towards bottling and sharing his wisdom."

- Teresa Mackintosh, Partner, Blue Star Innovation Partners;
Board Member, AvidXChange; former CEO, Trintech

"Mike Praeger is relentless in his pursuit of possibilities. He is a master at envisioning a compelling future and then bringing it into reality."

- Mike Whitehead, CEO and Founder, Center For Intentional Leadership

"When our company was at a critical stage in our development, Patrick and his team helped us understand the importance of vision, refine our mission, and emphasize the need for a system to manage our priorities. With their help, we grew into one of the largest and most respected staffing companies in America. I highly recommend Patrick and Michael's *The Journey to CEO Success* for anyone who wants to be a more effective and successful leader."

- Dr. Jay Cohen, Co-Founder, Dexian (formerly Signature Consultants)

"I have known Patrick and Michael for more than 10 years. The wisdom reflected in *The Journey to CEO Success* is not only a profound guide for leaders but also an embodiment of their collaborative genius, offering practical and effective strategies that are indispensable for any C-Level executive. This book no doubt will be celebrated by many for its actionable advice, and is a must-read for leaders wishing to enhance their journey with proven methods that have already paved the way to success for numerous C-Level executives."

- Geoff Gray, Chief Customer Relationship Officer, Dexian

"A leader's most important asset is clarity of purpose. The coaching and practices in this book have helped me develop my own purposeful leadership style with confidence. Use it to further develop your leadership brand and style!"

- Maruf Ahmed, President and CEO, Dexian

"I have had the pleasure of learning and applying the seven practices and I am a better leader for it, but more importantly, the companies I work with are better off for these practices. Read and apply."

- Mark Nussbaum, Chief Administrative Officer and Founder, Dexian (formerly Signature Consultants)

"If you want a company that executes at a high level and has a culture of people who care and perform, "Be Curious" and adopt these seven practices. It works!"

- Jeffrey C. Firestone, COO, Dutch Valley Family of Companies; President, Dutch Valley Food Distributors

"Patrick and Michael's collaborative effort delivers a profound guide with *The Journey to CEO Success*, offering invaluable insights for leaders navigating today's complex landscape."

- Stephen Shepard, CEO, Farmer Focus

"As an entrepreneur myself, and having been Michael Praeger's investment banker, investor, board member and friend since 2009, I've seen Mike in the trenches for nearly 15 years. Growing his business from $10mm in revenues to many hundreds of millions today, it is incredible to see Michael's core principles laid out for all to devour. This book is a masterclass in CEO leadership and a treasure trove for any entrepreneur on the journey to greatness."

- Steve McLaughlin, Founder and CEO, Financial Technology Partners

"Mike has led AvidXchange on an incredible journey as he has gone from founder to public company CEO. His unwavering dedication to creating a premier software as a service company in Charlotte, NC, and his focus on appropriately evolving his leadership style while building a high-performing leadership team, have driven the company to deliver outstanding sustainable growth. AvidXchange's success is clear evidence of Mike's vision, persistence and determination!"

- Lance Drummond, Chairman of the Board, Freddie Mac;
Board Member, AvidXchange

"Patrick's *The Journey to CEO Success* distills transformative insights into seven core practices essential for any serial entrepreneur aiming to scale new heights. A must-read for those committed to leading high-growth ventures with visionary zeal."

- Peter Stas, CEO, MMT and Founder, Frederique Constant

"Through practical advice and real-world examples, this book equips leaders at all levels with the tools and mindsets needed to navigate challenges and thrive in today's business environment. A must-read for anyone committed to personal and professional development."

- Sushant Trivedi, CEO, Fresh Tracks Canada

"These secrets are worth at least $150k/year of executive coaching. I have worked with Patrick for over 12 years and this feels like cheating!"

- Jorge Partidas, CEO, Globofran and Movigy

"Patrick and Michael know what it takes to build an incredible business and their techniques helped me do it too."

- Aaron Houghton, former CEO and Chairman, iContact

"Growth is my very top priority as a CEO and I found this book to be immensely helpful and inspirational in framing it with the leadership skills, disciplines and attitudes necessary to turn aspirational growth into real growth."

- Dave Cook, CEO, InsightOne

"Patrick's blueprint is a must-have for any CEO. I've had the privilege to implement his methodology across multiple businesses with great success."

- Krish V. Patel, CEO, KVP Inc.

"Mike is one of the most inspirational leaders of our time. Mike shares his tremendous knowledge and experience providing valuable insights to all who read this book. This is a must-read for any scaling entrepreneur."

- Asif Ramji, former CEO, Paymetric; Board Member, AvidXchange

"Michael's humility, drive and passion for constant personal growth — all qualities I deeply associate with him — are evident through the anecdotes in the book and 100 percent authentic to him as an entrepreneur. The path of a successful business, of a successful founder, is never linear. But through their hard-earned lessons, Michael and Patrick give leaders and aspiring leaders an outsized chance of kinking the curve on outcomes."

- Nigel Morris, Managing Partner, QED Investors; former Co-Founder, President, and COO, Capital One; former Board Member, AvidXchange

"These seven practices helped accelerate our capabilities to effectively plan and execute, which in turn helped us achieve our first audacious goal of putting 10 million pairs of shoes on children all over the world."

- Manny Ohonme, Founder and CEO, Samaritan's Feet International

"Having observed Mike's journey from industry pioneer to team motivator to master capital allocator has been a tremendously rewarding experience; the fact that he did it with constant positive energy and enthusiasm is a life lesson for us all."

- Bo Stanley, Partner and Co-Head, Sixth Street Growth; former Board Member, AvidXchange

"Mike is a visionary leader with unwavering tenacity coupled with a human-centric leadership style. His practical wisdom and guidance, captured in this book, will undoubtedly help shape the next generation of leaders."

"While new to working with us, Patrick has made a real difference. He has worked with me to give me confidence that by applying method, I can take on my greatest personal challenges. With our team as a collective we have applied the Rhythm method to bring greater execution precision with 'rhythmic' cadence, again imparting confidence through method. We are going through one of the most aggressive transformations a legacy company has embarked upon and Patrick will be a part of our collective success."

"A culture of performance emerges from a dedication to clear frameworks and disciplined processes. Patrick and Michael have distilled their extensive experience into practical and insightful advice for CEOs and aspirants. A must-read if you are a practitioner in the art and science of performance."

"Seven relevant and impactful practices that will really help me guide our company as we keep growing consistent with Patrick's Think, Plan, Do philosophy."

"As leaders in our companies, we need to always learn, improve, and grow to succeed in an ever-changing world. Thanks to Patrick and Michael for reminding me that it begins within US! As the CEO of our family business, I need to look in the mirror and say 'self, it starts with you'!"

- Brandon Tarbell, President and CEO, Tarbell Management Group

"Patrick clearly outlines the practices that will help any CEO grow their business. This book compresses a lot of wisdom into an easy-to-digest framework."

- Piers Carey, CEO, Teneo

"Patrick's work helped our leadership team align our efforts and contributed to our ability to achieve our strategic priorities. As CEO, Patrick's methodologies and insights were extremely important in the value the leadership created."

- Blaine Raddon, former CEO, The Channel Company

"Having known Patrick for more than ten years, I can attest that his strategies have significantly improved my capabilities and effectiveness as a CEO and leader."

- Sheldon Wolitski, Founder and Executive Chairman, The Select Group

THE JOURNEY TO CEO SUCCESS

PATRICK THEAN + MICHAEL PRAEGER

THE JOURNEY TO CEO SUCCESS

7 PRACTICES FOR **HIGH GROWTH LEADERSHIP**

Advantage | Books

Published by Advantage Books, Charleston, South Carolina.
An imprint of Advantage Media.

ADVANTAGE is a registered trademark, and the Advantage colophon is a trademark of Advantage Media Group, Inc.

Printed in the United States of America.

10 9 8 7 6 5 4 3 2 1

ISBN: 978-1-64225-852-3 (Hardcover)
ISBN: 978-1-64225-851-6 (eBook)

Library of Congress Control Number: 2024904032

Cover and layout design by Matthew Morse.
Illustrations by Nicole Thean.

This publication is designed to provide accurate and authoritative information in regard to the subject matter covered. It is sold with the understanding that the publisher is not engaged in rendering legal, accounting, or other professional services. If legal advice or other expert assistance is required, the services of a competent professional person should be sought.

Advantage Books is an imprint of Advantage Media Group. Advantage Media helps busy entrepreneurs, CEOs, and leaders write and publish a book to grow their business and become the authority in their field. Advantage authors comprise an exclusive community of industry professionals, idea-makers, and thought leaders. For more information go to **advantagemedia.com**.

CONTENTS

Over the last 30 years, I've invested in many companies, sat on many boards, and worked with many founders and CEOs. Occasionally, I've had the chance to work with an entrepreneur who can start a company, grow it sustainably, take it public, and continue scaling and leading the business to deliver strong and predictable results.

This seldom happens. Entrepreneurs tend to be successful up to a particular stage in their company's growth. Then, at some point, they stop being able to scale with the company and become their own most significant obstacle. The founder reaches a threshold where they must grow their leadership capabilities or step aside and bring in an experienced manager to scale the business to the next level. Many founders are uncomfortable and unprepared to transition away from the frontline work of product building and customer interaction to focus on business management.

I have had a front-row view of the leadership journey of Michael Praeger, beginning with his first software company in the 1990s in Boston. In 2014, I joined the board of AvidXchange, the software-enabled payments company Michael founded in 2000. Throughout my tenure on AvidXchange's board, I saw firsthand how Michael's relentless drive, passion to become a great leader, and curiosity enabled him to evolve and build his leadership capabilities while navigating through each growth and organizational milestone. During this period, AvidXchange experienced a 10X increase in revenue and became a public company with its IPO in October 2021.

The seven practices Michael learned during his journey—which you will find in this book—helped him dramatically increase his leadership effectiveness, achieve incredible growth, and build several billion dollars in shareholder value. Michael's growth was guided and accelerated by his coaching partnership with his long-time business advisor, Patrick Thean, who has worked relentlessly with Michael on his development journey. They aren't finished; Michael continues forward with the same motivation, drive, and curiosity to grow as a leader and take AvidXchange to its next milestone: achieving $1 billion in annual revenues and being the dominant industry player in their market segment.

To grow as Michael has, incorporate the seven practices discussed in this book into your ways of working and being. These practices must become deeply embedded habits since it takes repetition and discipline to grow as a leader. To build your organization, you must build yourself—and you must do so continuously.

Start with the foundational stages of self-development, captured in the first two practices shared in this book: Be Curious and Level Up. Curiosity will spur you to grow your knowledge, and a genuine desire to level up will open your eyes to daily growth opportunities. If you're not enacting these two practices, your leadership abilities are already becoming stale. Failure will creep in, unnoticed at first, and then seemingly multiply overnight. But very few failures happen overnight. Most took root long ago, but without curiosity and the drive to level up, you cannot see them until they're too big to correct.

This book will spark your curiosity to go deeper and further as a CEO, leader, and human being. It will help you avoid failure and repeatedly tackle new challenges and obstacles. Follow these practices to develop yourself, execute effectively, build a strong organizational culture, and serve your customers with excellence. Do these things, and you will increase your chances of success as a leader and a CEO.

I hope you will enjoy the seven practices that Michael and Patrick share and implement them in your growth journey.

–BRAD FELD
PARTNER, FOUNDRY

ACKNOWLEDGMENTS

PATRICK THEAN

The vision I had for this book became a reality thanks to the contributions of various family members, friends, partners, and peers in the business world. I owe my gratitude to the following people:

Colin Campbell, a close friend who also happens to be a serial entrepreneur and an author himself, most recently publishing *Start. Scale. Exit. Repeat.: Serial Entrepreneurs' Secrets Revealed!* Colin's work ethic is inspiring, but so is his willingness to reevaluate and re-strategize when necessary. He exemplifies leveling up.

Ratmir Timashev, co-founder of Veeam and a longtime client. As a leader, Ratmir inspires his people with the power of curiosity and strikes the balance between self-belief and humility—a harmony essential to great leadership.

The late Dr. Stephen Vogt, former CEO of BioPlus. The loss of Dr. Vogt in 2022 deeply impacted anyone who had the privilege to work with him—including me. His obsession with learning and his positive attitude always wowed me. He was a master at leading with purpose.

Sheldon Wolitski, founder of The Select Group. Sheldon acutely understands the value of coaching and uses it to stay grounded, accountable, and in touch with his authentic self.

Bob Potter, former CEO of SentryOne through their acquisition by SolarWinds. Bob masterfully demonstrates how to use feedback to grow as a self-aware leader.

Amy Ankrum, who led Qualtrax through a successful acquisition as CEO. Amy cares deeply about leveling up and catching her blind spots. She invests in herself and invests in her people.

Dr. Jay Cohen, who founded Signature Consultants and then merged his company with DISYS to create a billion-dollar staffing company called Dexian. Jay understands the need to reinvent oneself in the face of growth, and he seeks out honest feedback to help him on his journey.

Mort O'Sullivan, founder and CEO of ARCA. Mort listens and leans in to good advice and works tirelessly to meet and exceed his core customers' needs.

My Rhythm team, including Jessica Wishart and Katie Schmarr, who helped me edit and finalize this book.

Graham Dixon, who was invaluable in collecting content and writing alongside me.

Jeff Berstein, former CEO of ImageFIRST, who has shown commitment to growing his leaders. He provided an inspiring example of leveling up his leaders and improving his organization's culture.

Richard Giordanella, my first coach, who guided me on my journey to success. Without him, I would have never discovered my true calling of helping CEOs succeed.

Jaimie Petrie, my extraordinary executive assistant, who kept me on track throughout this process as this book's project manager. It is because of her that this book was finished and published!

My parents, Sally and LP Thean, who instilled in me the importance of honing my craft, and who inspired me to do my best in all that I do. My wife, Pei-Yee, who has accompanied me on my journey for the past 40 years. She curated my best stories for this book. My daughters, Joy and Nicole, for cheering me on and contributing their artistic talents. Nicole created the many wonderful illustrations you will see throughout this book.

MICHAEL PRAEGER

My partnership with Patrick for this book is an extension of a wonderful partnership that I have enjoyed with him for over 20 years. He was a trusted confidant at my side as I built AvidXchange into the industry leader and public company it is today.

My contribution became a reality thanks to my incredible AVDX teammates, all of my advisors and board members over the years, visionary investors, peers, and business coaches who all played a role in shaping the leader I am today and enabling me to scale my leadership capabilities from a start-up founder to a public company CEO. I owe my gratitude to the following people:

Mike Whitehead from the Intelligence Center of Leadership, along with Patrick Thean, were the catalysts for my development and challenged me to continue reaching for my next level of leadership capability so that I could ultimately become the CEO of an industry-leading public company.

Matt Harris of Bain Capital Venture Partners, who believed in my vision and energy to build an industry-leading company and gave me the heartfelt feedback I needed to hear to become a better leader each step of the way.

Nigel Morris of QED, who was always so gracious with his time and sharing his insights on all aspects of our business. His relentless focus on talent will forever be a key piece of our playbook in building AvidXchange.

Jim Hausman, a very wise, retired public company CFO, who has served as my longest tenured board member at AvidXchange and a true partner in helping me think through every crisis, acquisition opportunity, and new innovation that we scrimmaged in detail over the years.

Steve McLaughlin, a great friend, advisor, board member, and banker who helped me not only analyze, negotiate, and execute every acquisition and capital raise event after our founding of AvidXchange, but who also believed in my vision of what could be possible for AvidXchange.

Chris Coutinho, who is not only a great friend, but also inspired and supported me when I was 19 years old and a sophomore at Georgetown University to start a student painting business which proved to be the catalyst for the incredible entrepreneurial life journey I have been on ever since.

My Executive Team at AvidXchange, including Dan Drees (President), Joel Wilhite (CFO), Angelic Gibson (CIO and Technology Delivery Leader) and Todd Cunningham (Chief People Officer), who have been instrumental in helping me curate my annual personal development plan each year along with assembling the right advisors and coaches most relevant for each stage of our growth.

Laura Giffin, my longtime Personal Assistant who functions as my "voice" when I am not present and is truly an extension of myself in helping me be the best leader I can be.

My incredible family including my parents, Bob and Colleen Praeger, who were career educators and instilled in me the ability to dream about what's possible along with a work ethic which has enabled me to become the entrepreneur and leader I am today. My wife of 27 years, Cindy, who has always been my number one cheerleader and supporter in persevering even on my darkest days, along with my son, Chase, who is my daily inspiration to reach for the stars and continue my incredible life journey toward what could be possible.

CHAPTER 1

INTRODUCTION

My worst nightmare was becoming a reality: my company was about to die. And now, when I needed him the most, the one person I could ask for help was saying "no."

"Please just come down here," I remember begging him, "and see if you can help me."

"I don't think so."

"But ... I'm *dying* here," I told him.

"Nah," he said. "I don't want to come to Charlotte."

"Why not?" I asked, becoming more and more desperate. "I'll pay you for your time."

"I know," said Richard, "but I'm still not coming."

I pressed and pushed and begged, but he wouldn't budge. My lifeguard was flat-out refusing to throw me a life preserver. "Come down here, and assess things with me, just for a couple of days. *Please.*"

"Nope. Sorry."

"Why not?" I demanded again. I knew Richard enjoyed a flashy lifestyle—fancy meals and Ferraris. Guys like him usually like the idea of more money, right?

But he stuck to his guns. "I have all the clients I need here in New York," he explained. "There's just no reason for me to jump on a plane to Charlotte."

"Then I'm gonna *die*!" I reminded him.

"That's just panic."

"You *bet* I'm panicking!" I almost shouted. "You're going to read my company's obituary in the papers, and you'll know it was *your* fault!"

This wasn't the first time I'd been worried about Metasys. We'd already survived so many dangerous moments during our short history. Despite those, my company had grown quickly to $15 million in revenues and achieved Number 151 on *Inc. Magazine*'s Inc. 500 list of the fastest-growing privately held companies.

At that time, I believed we were facing challenges that threatened to kill our company. We'd already endured more than one cash crunch, hanging on only by our fingernails. We had to watch as our sales dipped and fight hard to regain sales success. And then there were personnel problems. I'd had to ask one of my partners to leave in our very first year, and when another left a few years later, I was convinced I'd need three people to replace her. In the end, it was only two, and again, we survived.

In difficult times, I'd managed to raise capital from investors to keep the lights on. My largest customer had asked to cancel their contract and demanded a $1.5 million refund, when at the time we were only a $2 million company. We successfully solved that crisis, and the customer not only remained a customer but also became a strong reference. What kept me going all those years was a desire to make a difference in the lives of our customers and our employees.

So, what was different about this time? Why was I on the phone to Richard, begging for help? After surviving so many crises, why was this one filling me with a sense of impending doom?

A lot of the pressure was coming from our venture capital partners and the fact that we had a high valuation. I had received offers to sell Metasys—including a prior offer from Richard himself as CEO of his previous company—and that only added to the stress. A high valuation sounds great, right? Not long before, an industry analyst had told me, "You're amazingly young to be so successful. If you cash out, you'd be financially set for life at age thirty!" But that's not how it felt to me. Selling at a high valuation was never my primary goal. I was a dream chaser and really wanted to build a great company that made a difference to the lives of people we touched—employees first, and then customers. But I felt like the dog chasing the car. Just as I got close, the car would get faster, and then where was I? Just a dog chasing a car again! That's how it felt to run a fast-growing company for the first time. Just as I thought I had learned enough to run it, it got bigger and faster. Things were starting to get away from me. And I was beginning to get exhausted.

Then, there were the day-to-day issues. Our customers were disappointed when we started getting late with product deliveries. We had more than sixty programmers, all working super hard, yet we were unable to deliver on time. Adding more engineers seemed to make us *less* efficient and *less* productive. And adding new features from customer requests added complexity. Our problems were multiplying.

Thanks to our having closed some large deals, Metasys was really taking off. But these new agreements included complex new features. No doubt these features made our software more compelling and unique, but we were having trouble delivering these features on time. In the software industry, this is known as "customer debt": features that were paid for and owed to customers. I took great pride in doing what I said I would do, and customers signed on believing in me and my team. As this customer debt began to pile up, I believed we were going to fail even though the company's financial performance continued to improve. This is because I believed that this compounding customer debt was a leading indicator of our company overcommitting, and unless we were able to get that under control and reduce our customer debt, we would ultimately fail. This caused me enormous stress and anxiety.

Then, at the height of our challenges, we won the Ernst & Young Entrepreneur of the Year award for North Carolina. But that only brought me even more stress!

My wife asked, "Why are you unhappy about winning this award? We're going to get great press for the company!"

I explained to her, "If Metasys had died last week, no one would have noticed. But now, if we go under, it will be a public disaster!"

All of this was weighing on me, adding a growing panic to the tone of my phone call to Richard. I also sounded tired, because I was. Not just regular tired but truly bone-deep tired. Years of hard work had left me so close to burnout that even my father had noticed, and he had set the example of working long and hard hours. As a lawyer in Singapore, he worked twelve-hour days, Monday to Saturday. He even worked Sunday mornings, though he was always home for our family lunch. He'd work in the evenings after dinner, and from my room next to his home office, I'd see that his light would stay on until midnight. And now, he was telling me to dial it back a little. "Careful, son," he told me, "you're working too hard."

"Yep, I sure am." I was proud of the hours I was putting in. "I'm working even harder than you did."

He agreed. "I never woke up at 6 a.m. and worked until 2 a.m. You're burning the candle at both ends."

"No," I proudly told him, "I'm burning it at both ends *and* in the middle!"

"You need rest," my father said. "Everyone does."

"Sleep is for the weak! I'll have lots of time to sleep when I am dead!" I said, making light of my crazy schedule.

Looking back, that sentiment feels pretty foolish. I was young and believed that hard work, drive, and energy could solve anything. Of course, I was being blind to the truth, persuading myself that I was a superhero who could work limitless hours without rest. "All I have to do," I told myself, "is to work harder than everyone else and *keep going*." But I really could not keep up this pace. I was starting to burn out.

I'd also started to resent how much people were asking of me—a classic early sign of burnout. The demands on me were relentless. I felt like a dish served on a lazy Susan, getting spun around while everyone took pieces out of me with their chopsticks. And for all my bullish talk—"I'll sleep when I die!"—people were starting to notice my growing exhaustion.

My cousin, Jiejun, visited me and noticed how tired I looked. "You know," she quipped, "watching you, I've learned that I don't want to be an entrepreneur. Some people have double bags under their eyes. But how the heck did you get triple-eye bags?"

It was around that time that I hit my limit. My company was set to implode. One hundred and eighty people were going to lose their jobs. Six years of the hardest work I'd ever done was going to yield nothing but failure. "I've 'Peter Principled,'" I told myself. "I've hit the limits of my competence. I should replace myself and hire a CEO to get us through this." I'm not a quitter, and the idea of bringing

5

in someone to help felt repulsive to me. But admitting that I needed help was a monumental realization. It's like going through addiction treatment: the first step is to acknowledge you've got a problem. I was addicted to my company, to growth, and to work. I'd become a workaholic and a growthaholic. It was time to reach out for some serious help. That's when I called Richard and begged him to come down to Charlotte.

What attracted me to Richard was his deep experience as a software CEO. He had taken two software companies public, and he was now advising various entrepreneurs. He sounded like the perfect advisor. With luck, he might even agree to come and run Metasys for me. But all I was hearing was, "No."

"Why not?" I asked.

And then, finally, he told me. "Remember a couple of years ago," he said, "when I offered to buy Metasys?"

"Yeah."

"Ever since then, I've had a nickname for you."

I could tell this wasn't going to be good. "Really?"

"Really. I call you 'Mr. X-Plus-One.'"

It clicked. "Oh."

"You remember now?"

I did, and his reluctance to help suddenly made perfect sense. "Uh-huh."

"I asked how much you wanted for Metasys," he said, warming to the tale, "and do you happen to recall your reply?"

I almost choked, painfully dredging up the overconfidence of a Patrick who was both much younger and *much* dumber. Eventually, I was forced to say, "Yeah. I said 'X-plus-one.'"

"And when I asked you what that meant, you replied, 'A buck more than you have, buddy!'"

Richard said, his voice filled with satisfaction.

Now, I felt about two inches tall.

"I complimented you by offering to buy your company. You could have said 'No' in a polite way, but instead, you insulted me. That is why I don't want to come to Charlotte to help you."

"I know. You are right. I was a jerk, and I'm sorry."

"And now," Richard said, clearly enjoying rubbing my face in it, "'Mr. X-Plus-One' has become 'Mr. I'll Die Without Your Help.'"

"Yeah." I'm glad to this day that our call took place before the days of Zoom, so Richard couldn't see the anguish and self-loathing on my face. "That's right."

"Oh, how the mighty have fallen," he intoned.

I asked him to forgive me and consider coming down to Charlotte to save me.

"Alright," he finally said. "I'll come down there."

"Really?" I said, brightening quickly. My lifeguard had finally seen that I was drowning. *And* he'd decided I was actually worth saving.

"Just three days, that's it," he promised. "Then we'll see what kind of shape you're really in."

We arranged for him to meet the Metasys executive team. In the days before his arrival, they were pretty freaked out. The rumor mill started up: "We're bringing in the ex-CEO of a successful public company? What's going on? Is Patrick fixing to replace himself?" Naturally, some worried that Richard would find that our problems were among our team and start to clean house. Any moment of change and uncertainty is scary, and this was no different.

At the end of the three days in Charlotte, Richard shared his thoughts. "Your problems are typical of a successful, high-growth software company. Your products are gaining momentum, and that brings problems. Right now, you don't have the experience to solve those problems, and so they feel a lot worse than they really are. But they're very solvable. It will take hard work, but you're no stranger to that," he told us. "You need more experience and some guidance to calm down, solve your issues, and reduce the chaos and stress." Then he told me, "Your people have their heads down. They're overworked but under-inspired. As for you, I know you've worked really hard, but you look haggard and depressed. You are not having fun anymore."

"Yep, I am," I replied candidly. "That's why I called you."

"There's nothing bad happening at Metasys," he told us all. "You're experiencing the problems of success. To you, it looks like chaos. But I've got more experience, and I can see the patterns. Sure, you've got customers who are yelling at you because you can't deliver what you promised, but no one delivers 100 percent of the time."

YOUR PROBLEMS ARE TYPICAL OF A SUCCESSFUL, HIGH-GROWTH SOFTWARE COMPANY.

Richard got us all into a room. "I want you to do an assets exercise." He had us write down all the positive things about our company and list all our assets. We were all exhausted and worn down by stress, so the list we wrote was very short. He facilitated our session: "Your customers are also positive assets. So, make a list of them."

When we were done, we looked at the combined list on the glass boards. Quickly, some optimism began to return. Our head of development said, "Wow! We have a pretty awesome list of assets!"

"Damn straight!" Richard agreed. "And that means we have a pretty awesome company here!" He smiled and asked, "Anyone notice something interesting about your customer list?"

After we all tried to guess the answer but failed, he did what great coaches do: he educated us again, showing us a pattern that we hadn't yet seen. "Most of your customers are Fortune 500 companies. I see Monsanto, Levi Strauss, Michelin, Cisco Systems, etc. This is an incredible list of customers—American icons—who believe in your products and what you are building. We have so much here to work with! Of course, they are mad at you when you don't deliver on time. But they have also committed to you and believe that your product is right for them. So, there's no need for self-pity," he told us. "Just look at this list of customers and your other assets. Look at it for as long as you need to. If you can't get excited about a list like that, I don't know what's wrong with you."

Then, he gave us a stern instruction. "When you leave this conference room, I want every one of you to be excited about solving all your problems. I want you all fully re-committed to building a great company together. And if you can't be excited, if you can't bring yourself to believe in this company, then we don't need you here!"

Richard hadn't said anything I didn't know, but he'd framed our situation so that my emotional brain could access it. First, he'd shown us a pattern that we hadn't been able to see: our incredible clients were our best assets, and listing them helped us to see that. Then, he'd spanked us for falling into the trap of assuming that our customers hated us and were ready to jump ship when, in fact, they needed us for their own success. We'd become defeatist and depressed, but Richard's perspective showed us that our situation was actually pretty favorable. Finally, he'd given us the inspiration we needed, a chance to reassess and re-engage, to come together and solve our problems.

When I spoke to him after the session, he said, "You've got a great company here. I know you've doubted that lately, but it's true. Your problems are typical of companies that grow fast and have great success. There's no reason to be scared. I've seen much worse problems than yours, and I promise they're solvable."

By this point, I was as impressed with Richard as I'd ever been with anyone. Right there and then, I asked him if he wanted to be our new CEO.

"I don't know," he answered. "But after three days here, I *do* know that you've got a great team, and they love you, but here's the strange thing: they don't view you as the boss."

This confused me. "How do you mean?"

"When you ask for something to be done," he commented, "they act like it's a suggestion. You don't hold them accountable for accomplishing the important things. You don't come back and check to make sure the execution is done. Plus, they're working hard for you, but they're not necessarily working on the right things." Then he said something else that really stuck with me. "I'm glad to report that you're not the arrogant jerk I thought you were. You're not really 'Mr. X-Plus-One'. In fact, you've demonstrated vulnerability working with your team. You've got the humility to admit that you need to learn and enough curiosity to learn and change. That's why your team loves you. You'll find those are key traits to being a successful CEO."

I liked him even more now, so I asked him again if he'd join us as our new CEO. If we stayed alive, Metasys seemed destined to become a great company, and any senior software executive would have found the position desirable.

This time, he refused. "I've enjoyed working with you. I always say that life is too short to work with people you don't like. You're one of the select few." That felt pretty good, but I still wanted him to come to Charlotte and drive the change we needed. "I'm not going to do that. Because I think you'd be missing a great learning opportunity if someone else came in here and solved your problems. I promised you three days, and I said I'd share my observations and my prognosis. I might consider coming to help you and guide you, every now and then. Help you tame this chaos. Share patterns with you that I have seen a hundred times and discuss how to solve your problems. But I don't want to make any emotional decisions today. Let me think about this some more and get back to you."

Looking back, I realized that Richard had coached me through my most difficult challenge at Metasys. Instead of taking the job as CEO when I offered it to him, he coached me and guided me in the following ways:

1. Encouraged me to move forward when I felt hopeless.
2. Inspired me by opening my eyes to the positive things we had achieved and the possibilities of our future.
3. Taught me how to calm down and solve critical problems instead of doing it for me. In other words, he taught me how to fish versus feeding me with fish. Over the years, I have come to also realize that this is the difference between coaches and consultants. Consultants are paid to catch and feed you fish. Nothing wrong with that. It's just good to know the difference.
4. Held me accountable to do what I promised.
5. Assessed my team and showed me how to lead and develop them with empathy and demanding performance at the same time.

When I recalled my time with Richard, it filled me with gratitude and respect. CEOs have a tough job, one of the toughest in the world.

It's not always fun, and it can be lonely at times. I was in a desperate and vulnerable place. He could have taken advantage of me, but he did not. Instead, he gave me empathy, coached me, and helped me to get back up to recapture the joy and excitement of running my company.

I realized that this is my true calling, my purpose: To help CEOs not fail but instead succeed, build great companies, and achieve their dreams.

MY TRUE CALLING, MY PURPOSE: TO HELP CEOS NOT FAIL BUT INSTEAD SUCCEED, BUILD GREAT COMPANIES, AND ACHIEVE THEIR DREAMS.

CHAPTER 2

MICHAEL PRAEGER

"I need help," my friend Michael Praeger told me. "I know the smartest person in technology, but he's too busy and too far away to help me. So, I'm asking you, the second smartest person I know in technology. How about it?"

"*Second* smartest?" I laughed. "If you're asking for help, shouldn't you tell me that I am the smartest technology person you know?"

"But if I told you that, I'd be lying!"

We both laughed, I said, "Sure!", and our journey together began.

Who could predict that twenty years later, I would introduce Michael to people as "the smartest and most successful financial technology (FinTech) entrepreneur and public company CEO whom I know personally"?

I had met Michael through the Entrepreneurs' Organization (EO), which was called Young Entrepreneurs' Organization (YEO) at that time. He was an active member of EO when he was running a software company based in Boston. However, Charlotte did not have an EO chapter when he moved here. As part of my desire to give back to my local entrepreneur community, I teamed up with

Stuart Meyerson (current VP of sales at Prime Therapeutics) to start the local EO Charlotte chapter as a way for Charlotte entrepreneurs to meet and learn from one another. We contacted Michael since he was already a member of EO International.

Michael and I ended up in the same forum and quickly became great friends. We soon discovered that we were on a similar journey and at similar crossroads: we were both successful entrepreneurs who had just sold our companies and were dreaming about our next startup. Michael had more startup experience, and he was already thinking about his fourth startup. Me? I just thought of myself as a software guy trying to figure out life.

Michael was on the verge of starting AvidXchange with his business partner, David Miller. Since then, AvidXchange has grown to be a public fintech company (Nasdaq symbol AVDX) that automates the accounts payable and payment process for over 8,800 middle market companies, along with building a business-to-business payment network with over one million suppliers.

Michael was the first entrepreneur and CEO whom I helped. Thanks to him, without realizing it, I had started my journey as a coach to CEOs and leaders of companies.

Early in our relationship, I could already see that Michael had the makings of a great leader. He had an insatiable appetite to learn and a humility that disguised his successful track record. He had already grown and sold three companies, yet he continues to seek personal growth and development. The best leaders do not allow their success to turn them into someone who is proud and unapproachable. Instead, they maintain their humility and their hunger to learn.

I WAS INSPIRED BY STORIES OF STEVE JOBS TAKING WALKS WITH HIS COACH, BILL CAMPBELL, AND HOW THESE INFORMAL DISCUSSIONS HELPED STEVE JOBS WRESTLE AND WORK OUT HIS BIGGEST QUESTIONS.

I was inspired by stories of Steve Jobs taking walks with his coach, Bill Campbell, and how these informal discussions helped Jobs wrestle and work out his biggest questions. From the beginning, I modeled our coaching sessions after this. Over the years, our coaching sessions have had this informal "walk in the woods" feeling. Michael would update me on the business, and we would discuss the number one thing on his mind. We would reflect on his actions and the resulting outcomes, discuss possible solutions to opportunities as well as challenges, and agree on the action plans that he would take. By sharing his action plans with me, our process created a bias for action with commitment and accountability. We have met every month for the last twenty-three years. This has given Michael a consistent and dependable rhythm of lifting his head up from the day-to-day operational work to spend time thinking and working on the business.

One of our coaching sessions took place a few days after he'd endured a very difficult board meeting. He was discouraged. "Everyone there thinks that I am a terrible leader. They said that I need to figure out how to grow my leadership capabilities to keep up with the growth of AvidXchange, or we will fail."

"Take a look at this." I drew a basic graph on the whiteboard. "The vertical line is the leadership scale, from 'good' at the top to 'bad' at the bottom. This horizontal line across is the 'normal' level of leadership—think of it as the average of all leaders. OK. Now, go ahead and place an 'X' on the board where you think you are as a leader."

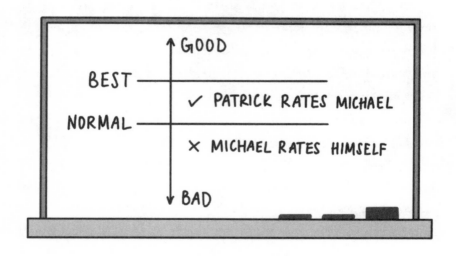

"About … there." I wasn't surprised when he marked his "X" well below the "normal" line.

"OK, wait a minute," I said. "You have a successful company. AvidXchange has already eclipsed $4 million in annual recurring revenues, and you have approximately thirty employees who believe in you." I could tell that he'd lost sight of those achievements and felt beaten down by his board's characterization of his performance. "Your teammates are willing to follow you into battle. That proves that you don't suck," I told him. "In fact, you're pretty good. You just need to figure out how to scale your own leadership capabilities to the next level."

I drew another line, well above the zero-line. "Here's where the best leaders are. And here," I said, adding an "X" halfway between the two, "is where you are now. You're above 'normal,' but you're not yet the best. But you don't suck. So, let's work on getting to the next level."

Michael pondered the diagram for a while. Then he smiled and said, "OK, let's get to work." Never one to sidestep doing the hard work, he asked, "What do I need to do to get to the next level?"

In a relationship as long and fruitful as ours, we have walked through numerous high points and low points together. AvidXchange has gone through many pivotal moments during its successful journey from startup to Unicorn (privately held company valued at more than US$1 billion) to public company on the Nasdaq stock exchange.

In addition to our monthly coaching sessions, Michael and I also ran quarterly planning sessions that enabled his executive team to extract themselves from the day to day to think and plan for the next quarter. These have been immensely valuable. When time is tight and there's a lot on their plates, it's tempting to skip one, but they never have. Each session provides Michael and his executive team with time to think about and examine the business, allowing them to see the forest from the trees and identify root causes. This has given them a cadence that helps them get ahead of issues so that they can prevent fires instead of fighting fires.

In October 2021, Michael successfully took AvidXchange public, creating a $700 million war chest for the company. As we celebrated and hugged after his successful initial public offering (IPO), I was reminded of a scene from one of my favorite movies, *Jerry Maguire*. Jerry was Rod Tidwell's sports agent. Toward the end of the movie, Rod catches the game-winning touchdown but suffers a terrible collision and is knocked unconscious in the process. Thankfully, he recovers and celebrates his winning moment on the field. Jerry greets him later when he emerges from the locker room. They hug, Rod tells Jerry, "We did it!", and Jerry corrects him: "You did it!"

Michael and I have had this wonderful relationship over the last twenty-three years. Our journey continues in the writing of this book and beyond. I am thrilled that he has collaborated with me as my co-author. He is passionate about using his real-life experience to help other CEOs and leaders achieve breakthroughs, succeed, and fulfill their dreams.

CHAPTER 3

WHY YOU NEED THIS BOOK

"If you want a guarantee, buy a toaster."

–CLINT EASTWOOD

WHY THIS BOOK?

The journey of a CEO or any senior leader is tough. I have had the privilege of walking with and coaching CEOs for over twenty years. During this journey, I have learned that leading and making the right decisions are hard. I have witnessed many leaders make poor decisions without realizing it or considering the opportunity costs. When we zoom out over three or five years, we see in hindsight how dear some of these mistakes were.

Your journey as a leader will be filled with challenging yet exhilarating twists and turns. I am not suggesting that mistakes are all bad. In fact, I applaud the speed and courage necessary to make decisions that might end up being mistakes. However, we all need the right practices to identify these wrong decisions and correct them quickly.

This book is meant to help you make smarter decisions, be a better leader, and make corrections faster.

You are on a special path. Michael and I want to help you have a more fulfilled and successful journey.

UNCOMMON LEARNINGS

There really isn't a cookbook or formula that can guarantee success. As Clint Eastwood said, "If you want a guarantee, buy a toaster." Often, a one-size-fits-all approach applied without full understanding of the situation leads to failure instead of success. Any insight shared in this book needs to be considered together with the unique situation in front of you and the unique group of people you are working with, and then fine-tuned or personalized, to be truly useful.

After thousands of coaching sessions, Michael and I have curated seven very important practices that have helped many CEOs achieve major breakthroughs. We are focused on noticing and articulating uncommon learnings from the stories that our friends have been kind enough to allow us to share.

At the start of each chapter, we will share the main takeaways. There is no need to keep you in suspense! If you don't like reading stories, you may read the first section of the chapter, fast-forward to the "Bottom Line" points at the end of the chapter, think on these takeaways, and move on to the next chapter. However, many readers might discover a deeper understanding from the specific application of each practice. If you fall into this category, please enjoy the stories that capture the nuances of real-life situations. You just might discover important patterns as you apply these practices to your own circumstances.

WHO IS THIS BOOK WRITTEN FOR?

This book is for leaders and aspiring leaders. Yes, the title of the book specifically calls out CEOs. Yet, these seven practices apply to the journeys of all leaders. More specifically:

- You are the CEO of a growth company, and you need to lead your various stakeholders (employees, customers, board members, investors) and inspire them with hope and vision. You need to drive execution and achieve breakthroughs to achieve results and be successful.
- You are a senior executive experiencing change that might feel unsettling, and you need to lead your team by making the right decisions to give them confidence in the future of the company.
- You are a manager who needs to understand how decisions are made by the senior executives in your company and equip yourself to support these decisions.
- You are an aspiring leader who wants to learn more by understanding how decisions are made to level up for future leadership opportunities.
- You are a consultant who coaches CEOs or senior executives, and you want to gain more insight and expertise to help your clients achieve success.

THE JOB

Jack was an experienced CEO focused on giving his investors a successful financial exit. He had led his company to achieve good financial results over the last few years and prepared a plan for the next stage of growth for new investors to consider.

After successfully selling the business to new investors, Jack settled in to execute the growth plan with them. However, after a few quarters, his company started to fall short of the targets committed to in the growth plan. Then, in 2020, COVID happened, and the firm's growth slowed down further. Jack gave his investors an honest appraisal: the aggressive plan wasn't going to work, and he needed to re-forecast.

The investors listened to the revised plan, and even though they were not pleased, to Jack's relief, they agreed to it. This was a much less aggressive version that took global events into account. He worked hard with his executive team, and they finished the year achieving their revised targets.

Then, Jack got the call. The investors fired him.

"But ... I achieved our revised targets!" he said to himself, shocked at this development. "I was honest with the investors. I didn't pull any stunts or lie to anyone. I kept them in the loop all the way through. And," he lamented, "they all *agreed* to the revised plan."

Jack had to learn the hard lesson that hitting re-forecasted targets was not good enough. He was replaced because he was not able to meet the original targets. Those targets were commitments. Missing commitments has serious consequences, and Jack was replaced as CEO.

This is a rather common story. It does not seem fair. It's a job fraught with difficulties, and sometimes, even if you feel you've done your absolute best, you can still end up getting fired. It is a tough yet exhilarating job. It's the job all CEOs signed up for. Here are some sobering statistics about the job of CEO:

- The chances of a CEO being fired tripled between 1970 and 2006.
- Between 1984 and 2000, the chances of a CEO keeping their job for ten years fell by 60 percent.
- Only 50 percent of CEO departures are voluntary.

- CEO firings, though more common than before, rarely result in a major turnaround for the company. Often, they prove to have been a knee-jerk reaction from investors reacting to poor financial news, are poorly handled by the company's board, and fail to reassure the markets. But that doesn't mean they're going to happen less often.

ENRICH YOUR JOURNEY—DON'T STOP WITH THIS BOOK

This book is the third in the Rhythm series. To learn more about tried-and-true methods that help leaders execute their strategy with accountability, read these other titles:

- *Rhythm: How to Achieve Breakthrough Execution and Accelerate Growth* (a *USA Today* and *Wall Street Journal* Best Seller)
- *Predictable Results: How Successful Companies Tackle Growth Challenges and Win*

CHAPTER 4

THE SEVEN PRACTICES

"Practice is the price you pay today to be better tomorrow."

–JAMES CLEAR

When I sold my first company, Metasys, I was more burned out than I'd thought was possible. But I had some time to reflect, and I saw that two things were true. Leading and growing the company had felt like a never-ending journey of solving crisis after crisis, one near-impossible escape after another. But viewed from the outside, the company was a huge success. After I sold the company, many entrepreneurs approached me for help and advice. I tried my best to help.

I have spent the last twenty-plus years helping leaders succeed. In doing so, a number of patterns became clear and evident. This book captures the most important patterns that my team and I have experienced with our customers on their way to success. Their stories may be different, but thankfully, the patterns are similar. I hope the seven practices captured in this book will help you navigate your way toward success.

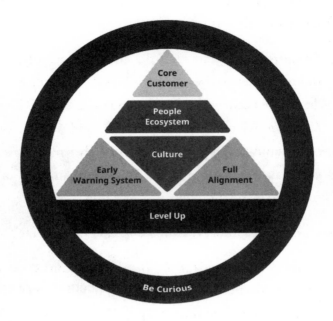

THE 7 PRACTICES

First, we need to start with ourselves. I've had a few calls with CEOs asking for assistance that go something like this: "Patrick, I would like you to visit us, interview my executive team, and help me figure out who should go and who should stay. They are not executing well as a team, and it is really frustrating for me!"

I reply, "How do you know it's them and not you? In my experience, the fish usually rots from the head down."

A long pause follows.

The answer from the CEO may be along the lines of, "OK, let's start with me. If I am the problem, then please help me fix me. And if not, please help us get better as a team." That's a step in the right direction, and I might just have a new customer. If the CEO insists that their team is the problem, that's when I know that I'm not the right person to provide assistance.

The first two practices help us lay a strong foundation for success by working on ourselves as leaders:

1. *Be Curious:* We start with the circle of curiosity. Curiosity should encompass everything we do. We will explore the difference between BEING curious and DOING curious.

2. *Level Up:* We need humility to learn and improve ourselves continuously. Whenever we find ourselves blaming someone else or unfortunate circumstances, we are missing an opportunity to learn and grow.

Then we need to improve how we get the work done:

3. *Establish Your Early Warning System:* If we can't see it, we can't avoid it. We need an early warning system to alert us before we get smacked on the side of the head.

4. *Achieve Full Alignment:* Work gets done and delivered in teams. If we are still operating in silos, we are in for a world of hurt! We need to get the most out of our teams in a joyful way.

Next, we need to make sure we have created the right environment for our teams to be successful:

5. *Make Culture Your Competitive Advantage*: This is the practical side of culture. Our working culture sets the right environment for us and our teams to succeed. When we do culture right, we significantly improve our Return on Payroll (ROP). When we do culture wrong, we are helping our competition beat us every day.

6. *Build a Strong People Ecosystem*: This is one of the toughest practices—to continually grow and renew our teams' skills.

Handled right, our people are our greatest assets. Ignored, our people become our heaviest anchors.

Finally, we need to fine-tune our strategy to focus on our core customer:

7. *Focus on Serving Your Core Customer:* Not all customers are equal. Some are more important than others—our core customers. We need to figure out who our core customers are and build our businesses to serve them and care a little less about the other customers. Marketing experts might call this "positioning to a niche category." However, this goes beyond positioning. This is about making decisions that prioritize this type of customer over all other customers, in all areas of the business.

These practices encompass elements of leadership, personal development, strategic thinking, and execution abilities. In the chapters that follow, we will delve into each practice and learn from the real-life experiences of CEOs who have used these practices to achieve success.

CHAPTER 5

BE CURIOUS

"The important thing is not to stop questioning.
Curiosity has its own reason for existing."

–ALBERT EINSTEIN

Let me start with a story that illustrates the power of curiosity. I was facilitating a planning session for Colin Campbell and Hostopia fifteen years ago. At that time, Hostopia was a leading provider of private-label web services and business communication tools. For over a decade, Hostopia had collaborated with the most successful companies in the areas of telecommunications and media to activate new sales channels and generate new revenue streams. They were also a public company trading on the Toronto Stock Exchange. So you can imagine the stress Colin was feeling when he shared that they were short of their sales numbers by $10 million! As a public company, achieving published sales goals is nonnegotiable if you want to keep your stock price up. Failure to deliver would cause their stock price to fall and reduce their market valuation drastically.

"OK, so let's set aside time during this planning session to brainstorm sales ideas and solve this sales problem," I suggested.

"Yes, but I have already done that with my sales team, and we are still short by about $10 million," Colin told me.

I suggested that we try again and that he and his team activate their curiosity gene. I asked them to consider ideas that they might have easily dismissed before. Instead of thinking, "We have considered that, and it won't work," they should be curious and ask, "What do I still not know about this idea being proposed?"

Colin agreed, and we began a simple exercise I call "Twenty Ways." "We're going to find twenty ways to increase sales. Curiosity is key," I emphasized. "I want us to consider any and all options, including those we've previously thrown out. We will write these ideas on the board, and we won't stop until we have at least twenty ideas."

"What about killing the bad ideas?" asked an executive team member.

"No, we are not stopping to kill any ideas," I replied. I then shared the process:

1. Activate your curiosity gene.
2. Write down all ideas. Do not stop until there are at least twenty ideas.
3. Do not stop to assess or discuss any ideas.
4. Do not judge or kill any ideas. There are no bad ideas while brainstorming.

Stopping to discuss the validity of ideas will stop the flow of ideas. Judging or killing ideas during the brainstorming can cause participants to get hesitant and stop sharing ideas that they think are not good enough. Sometimes, great ideas come on the backs of ideas that might not work. So by judging and removing ideas from the list during brainstorming, we remove the catalysts that might give birth to good ideas.

And away we went! Twenty ways to generate an extra $10 million of sales before the year ends. I urged everyone to ask more questions. Ask, "What do I not already know about this idea?" when an old idea is listed instead of assuming that the old idea will not work. By asking what we did not yet know, we injected curiosity into the process.

It started slow, but we kept going. I kept reminding the team to ask what they did not yet know, and more ideas began to flow. We started having fun and laughing at some of the crazy ideas that were suggested. When we finished, we had more than thirty-five ideas on the board. Colin was pleasantly surprised by the list of ideas.

We then analyzed and assessed these ideas. When we culled the list down into the top eight to ten ideas to do, we had $12–15 million of possible sales opportunities.

This lesson is not about this simple "Twenty Ways To" exercise. Rather, actively and intentionally being curious changed the exercise to allow the team to see what they could not see before. The same exercise done without intentionally applying curiosity would not have yielded these results.

ACTIVELY AND INTENTIONALLY BEING CURIOUS CHANGED THE EXERCISE TO ALLOW THE TEAM TO SEE WHAT THEY COULD NOT SEE BEFORE.

I am sure you are curious to know if Colin made his number that year. While not all the ideas panned out, those that did helped him achieve his stated goals. They ended the year successfully!

CURIOSITY IS THE NECESSARY INGREDIENT IN EVERYTHING YOU DO

Being curious can do so much for you. This chapter will explore how curiosity can help you:

1. become a good listener and accelerate learning,
2. build stronger relationships,
3. be a better boss,
4. hire the right talent,
5. use experience as a multiplier,
6. identify and solve the right problem, and
7. replace fear with curiosity.

Curiosity is the circle in this system, because it applies to every situation and decision that we have in front of us. If you choose to be curious in the moment, you will have better outcomes.

IF YOU CHOOSE TO BE CURIOUS IN THE MOMENT, YOU WILL HAVE BETTER OUTCOMES.

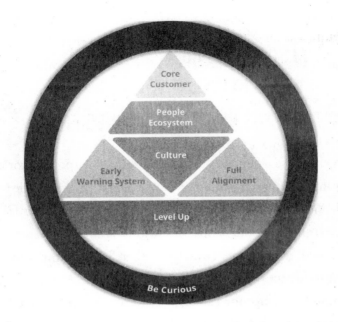

WHY IS CURIOSITY HARD?

The World Steals Our Curiosity

All of us are born curious, but the world extinguishes our curiosity. This starts with most of our teachers and parents, who encourage us to conform to societal norms. Our parents did the best they could with what they knew. They didn't realize that by quieting a curious child, they were discouraging us from being curious. By asking us to play less and make less noise, they were slowly teaching us that it was not acceptable to be playful and noisy. Those of us who continue to be playful and curious may then have been labeled as troublemakers. As we grow up through our teenage years, the world teaches us that we need to conform to social norms to do well in school, at work, and in our personal lives.

ALL OF US ARE BORN CURIOUS, BUT THE WORLD EXTINGUISHES OUR CURIOSITY.

It gets worse when we start working in the corporate world. Now our world is filled with people on a tight schedule, with little patience for reflection and downtime. Those who are more ambitious have even less time to ask questions, be curious, and play. The scramble to win the race, to get there (wherever "there" is), prompts us to keep our blindfolds on and rush to get things done. As we continue to succeed and develop our careers, we are rewarded for our behavior with promotions and salary increases.

Then one day, at the height of our success, we see cracks in our foundation and way of working. Those who see these cracks and wonder if something might be amiss are the lucky ones. They might pause and rediscover the importance and joy of being curious.

Those who ignore their gut instinct and push on have missed an opportunity to re-engage their curiosity gene. And that's OK. Fortunately, life often presents us with multiple opportunities to see what we need to see.

Knowledge Dampens Curiosity

Knowledge and experience also play a part in dampening our curiosity. When we do not understand something, we seek to learn. We ask questions. We explore. This is being curious.

As we become knowledgeable and more experienced in our fields of study and work, we gradually become experts. We begin to naturally ask less questions and dispense more advice. As we become more knowledgeable, unless we choose to be curious with intention, we lose curiosity over time. Unless we take time for self-reflection, we might not even notice this pattern. We do not realize that our success is driving curiosity out of our mindset.

In his 2008 book *Outliers*, Malcolm Gladwell wrote that "ten thousand hours is the magic number of greatness." His theory is that to be considered elite and truly experienced within a certain craft, you must practice it for ten thousand hours. I think of this also as ten thousand attempts or opportunities to practice.

Unfortunately, regarding curiosity, Malcom Gladwell's theory can be applied in a negative way. With each of those ten thousand hours, you have likely become less and less curious about your craft. You may have mastered your field, but you have also become a master in not being curious.

WITH EACH OF THOSE TEN THOUSAND HOURS, YOU HAVE LIKELY BECOME LESS AND LESS CURIOUS ABOUT YOUR CRAFT.

Familiarity kills curiosity. You've probably heard the phrase "Familiarity breeds contempt." If you know a person or situation very well, you can easily lose respect for that person or become careless in certain situations.

After working with your team for many years, it's easy to get familiar and anticipate what they are about to say or do. Instead of listening, we begin to hear what we expect them to say. Our minds begin to drift. We whip out our cell phones while the person is talking without realizing that we have lost interest. "I am sorry, I got distracted" might be the apology. If you were more self-aware, you would say, "I am sorry. I was no longer curious because I thought that I could predict what you were going to say."

HOW CURIOSITY CAN HELP YOU

I stated earlier that all of us are born curious. Let's talk about how to activate your curiosity gene and be a better leader.

Become a Good Listener and Accelerate Learning

One of the most common requests I get from CEOs and executive leaders is to help them become better listeners.

Jane (I often use "Jane" or "Jack" to allow my clients to contribute anonymously in this book) shared with me that her CEO 360 feedback survey had "Listening" as an area for her to improve as a leader.

"I have tried everything, Patrick!" she told me. "I've turned off my laptop in meetings, I've put my cell phone down face down, I am applying what I have learned about active listening. Yet, the feedback this year about me not listening well remains no different from last year."

"Jane, have you done this in 100 percent of your meetings with team members?" I asked.

"Well, not 100 percent. That would be impossible. When an urgent text or call comes in from a client or team member in the field, I have to respond. People must understand that! But I can tell you these interruptions are significantly less than the year before. I did not expect a perfect score, but to have people say that there is no improvement is really discouraging."

Jane tried really hard. She had done her best. Here's the thing about active listening—yes, it is a good skill, a good practice, and a "must" for all of us. But if you peel back the onion and look at the root cause, there are really two parts to listening: (1) the speaker needs to feel that they were heard, and (2) the receiver needs to have heard the message. When team members ask leaders to be better listeners, oftentimes it's because they do not feel heard.

To become a truly skilled listener, the simple solution is to activate your curiosity gene. You have to get curious about the topic and what the person is trying to communicate with you. Jane and I explored what being curious means in this situation.

- What is it about the topic that she does not yet know?
- Why was it important for her to be curious about the solution being presented?
- What questions might she ask that would help her understand better?

Think back to a time when you were really excited about a subject. Remember how you felt, how interested you were, and how excited you were about learning. You probably had no trouble paying attention to the speaker. Your ears perked up, and you applied all the skills of active listening without even realizing it. You paid attention. You listened with bated breath. You probably even caught the tiny nuances that other, less engaged people in the audience missed. And you were excited like a child when you discovered something you did not yet know. When you're interested in what you're learning, your curiosity becomes engaged naturally.

Here's the secret: choose curiosity. Yup. That's right. You can do this by simply choosing to be interested in a topic. Start with one question: "What is it about this topic that I do not yet know?"

BE CURIOUS—DON'T DO CURIOUS.

Go from unintentional curiosity to intentional curiosity. In this way, you will start to BE curious, not DO curious. What does this mean? *Being curious* means feeling genuine interest toward a person or topic. It starts with figuring out why you should be interested. Through that interest, you will become a fully present and engaged learner. *Doing curious* means applying certain techniques and skills—like active listening—in an attempt to learn. It is not bad to apply these techniques and skills, but if you are not genuinely interested, your learning will not be as rich.

START WITH ONE QUESTION: "WHAT IS IT ABOUT THIS TOPIC THAT I DO NOT YET KNOW?"

You can't really fake curiosity by following a checklist of behaviors. Most of the time, being curious is a choice. It's an intention. When you ask, "What is it about this topic that I do not yet know?" you trigger yourself to be curious. You figure out *why* you should be interested. It takes practice and discipline to consider this question over and over—of course it does! This may be simple, but it is not easy.

I have been Michael Praeger's coach for over twenty-three years. We have had over three hundred coaching sessions together. How do I not get tired or bored meeting with Michael and vice versa? I walk into every coaching session by being curious. I ignite my curiosity with this one question: "What is it about Michael Praeger that I do not yet know?" I get excited because I believe Michael will teach me something new. Being curious to learn is a choice. If you choose to learn, you will learn something new. Learning does not happen by chance. That's why we refer to people who are really serious about learning as knowledge-seekers. They are not knowledge-happeners, are they? No, they are knowledge-seekers!

Build Stronger Relationships

Jane updated me a year later and thanked me for helping her become a much better listener. Being curious positively improved her CEO 360 survey in the area of listening. I asked her what else she had learned. Did she notice any other benefits with this approach? What did this practice or question teach her that she did not know before?

As she reflected on this, she realized that in addition to becoming a better listener, her relationships with her team members had also improved! Wow... a two-for-one deal!

When we meet someone new and important, many of us make the mistake of trying too hard to be interesting in our desire to create a great first impression. I have discovered that trying to be interesting and attractive to the other person does not work as well as being truly interested in learning about the other person. If you can be curious and sincerely interested to learn about the other person, your interest will feel like a gift.

I experienced this gift years ago at the Ernst and Young's Entrepreneur of the Year Conference. Debbie Fields (founder of Mrs. Fields Cookies) was a keynote speaker at this conference. I was totally blown away by her speech. I found the way she recruited talent for her company unique and interesting. I became curious and hoped that I would find a way to meet her and learn more during the conference. Later that day, by sheer chance, I saw her walking toward me with her entourage. I could not believe how lucky I was. I decided to position myself so that our paths would cross.

When we came face-to-face, I very nervously thanked her for her keynote and asked if I might ask her a question. Her entourage glared at me. But she did not. She stopped, smiled, and asked me what my name was, what type of business I was building as an entrepreneur, and how she could help me. She gave me 100 percent of her attention and showed interest and, yes, even demonstrated curiosity about me. That was a memorable moment, not because she was interesting but because she was interested in me. She gave me the gift of her attention. Her interest in me made me feel special and important.

Philosopher John Dewey said, "The deepest urge in human nature is the desire to be important." When you are curious about someone, your curiosity translates into sincere interest that makes the person feel special and important. This might explain why when Jane learned how to be curious about her team members, she also became better at building relationships. Be curious, be interested in others, and your relationships will improve.

BE CURIOUS, BE INTERESTED IN OTHERS, AND YOUR RELATIONSHIPS WILL IMPROVE.

BE A BETTER BOSS

Being a better boss has everything to do with developing a better and stronger relationship with your employees. There is no ten-step process for this. There is just a one-step process: you've got to care more. That's it. Be curious, get interested, and care more.

The Gallup poll taught us that people don't quit companies—they quit people. Gallup has a set of questions called the Q12 that have been validated across 2.7 million people. One of the prompts is: "My supervisor, or someone at work, seems to care about me as a person." Bottom line: If you do not care about your employees, they will leave you! And they won't tell you the truth during an exit interview.

I have had too many leaders tell me that their employees left because of reasons unrelated to their leadership. I am sure they did leave for other reasons; however, there is also a good chance that they left *you* at the same time. Be curious and lean in. During an exit interview, instead of asking what they did not like about their manager, ask them what it was like working for that manager. Learn how to help the manager grow as a leader. People leave people. Wake up to the reality that the person who quit left their manager, not the company.

If the employee who chose to leave was part of the team you lead, listen hard to improve yourself. Even if they insist it was for a better job or opportunity, probe further: "And what was it like for you to work with me? How could I have inspired you more? Or helped you more?" Don't allow yourself to be a victim of the other person's opportunity or better job. You learn nothing as a victim. Own it to grow as a leader.

YOU LEARN NOTHING AS A VICTIM. OWN IT TO GROW AS A LEADER.

Caring about your employees as people, not as work assets, is important. It's important to them, and it should be important to you. You should do it because you want to be a better person. And if that does not inspire you, then do it to reduce your cost of employee attrition.

Be curious. Get interested in your employees. Be a better boss.

HIRE THE RIGHT TALENT

MICHAEL'S PERSPECTIVE

AvidXchange has grown rapidly over the last twenty-two years, and we're now a public company with over eighteen hundred employees. By the time this book is published, we will probably have more than two thousand employees. Needless to say, between my first three startups and AvidXchange, I have had to hire a lot of team members as well as correct mistakes when I hired the wrong people. Along the way, I have learned how important it is to hire curious people.

I hired two top executives, both seasoned with experience from great companies. They both appeared very similar when we interviewed them. Both impressed me and our entire executive team with their experience, knowledge, connections, and presence. I expected them to thrive in our culture at AvidXchange.

They arrived and started strong, jumping right in and asking lots of questions. Both brought with them methods and systems that they trusted and that had made them successful. They had pleasant personalities and also demanded results. We immediately felt the positive effect of both hires.

Let's talk about how Jack and John were different (like Patrick, I will use "Jack" and "John" to share my learnings while protecting the identities of these two men). Let's start with Jack. He turned out to be the executive who demonstrated less curiosity. Jack brought with him strong operational experience and a successful track record from multiple large companies. He demonstrated curiosity and interest when he assessed AvidXchange. Once he completed his assessment, he began to implement his processes and methods. But as he got more comfortable over time, he began to rely more on his experience and methods instead of continuing to be curious and asking why we would do things the way we did them.

For example, we use the Rhythm Think, Plan, Do methodology that Patrick teaches. It has been the framework for us to systematically come up with winning move strategies, translate them into annual and quarterly priorities in a way that allows us to focus, align our teams, and be accountable to execute. This process has been fundamental to our success as it prompts us on a weekly basis to proactively examine if we need to have any critical discussions to make sure projects and goals are on track. It helps us focus on meeting our commitments.

Jack did not dismiss the Rhythm framework. However, he did have confirmation bias toward methods that he was already experienced and comfortable with. He learned the framework but missed key components that did not conform to what he expected in areas that were different from what he was used to.

There's a big difference between being truly curious and Jack's way of learning. He only learned as much as he needed to apply systems that he was already familiar with. But curiosity goes so much further. It's about asking yourself what you don't yet know, because that's what bites you. We were a growing company in a nascent industry, so a thirst for filling knowledge gaps will hugely increase the chances of success.

John is very similar to Jack in many positive ways. However, curiosity sets them apart. John approached things with less confirmation bias. He was open to exploring how things might be different and valuable. He was open to learning what it was that had made AvidXchange so successful in the past. At the same time, he was unsatisfied with the status quo. Our best leaders do this at AvidXchange. They are able to hold two competing options in their minds without immediately dismissing one of them. They are able to examine both concepts, be curious, and create a third or fourth option that captures the best of both. Patrick calls this the power of the A-N-D. Instead of binary thinking or dualistic thinking and forcing a choice between A and B, find a way to be curious and take the best parts of A and B to create another option that is often stronger than the two original choices.

POWER OF THE A-N-D. INSTEAD OF BINARY THINKING OR DUALISTIC THINKING AND CHOOSING A OR B WHEN FACED WITH TWO CHOICES, FIND A WAY TO BE CURIOUS AND TAKE THE BEST PARTS OF A AND B TO ANOTHER OPTION THAT IS OFTEN STRONGER THAN THE TWO ORIGINAL CHOICES.

For John, curiosity and humility formed a powerful combination. He pushed deeper, seeking to understand. In doing so, he showed interest in the people and existing processes that we were using. He gained the respect of existing employees, which helped him become an effective leader. His combination of existing knowledge plus a thirst for new findings allowed him to discover new opportunities that others had missed. This was the power of his curiosity.

The uncommon learning here is to be curious first before applying your experience. Experience is what we all desperately need in young growth companies. Personally, I learned that I must hire for curiosity

and experience. Most leaders start with their experience and then use curiosity to fill in the blanks. I have discovered that doing the reverse leads to faster learning, stronger teamwork, and better results. In other words, first be curious and try to learn what you don't yet know. Then apply your experience on top of the new knowledge that came from being curious.

USE EXPERIENCE AS A MULTIPLIER

As we hired more people at AvidXchange, we really focused on experience. Since the company was growing so fast, we wanted people who had already walked the path we were on to help us all level up. If we are not learning as fast or faster than the rate of growth of the business, we will quickly be obsolete and replaced. But not everyone with strong experience and a successful track record succeeded. I believe the difference was being curious. I noticed that those who demonstrated humility, vulnerability, and curiosity to learn were able to apply what they learned as a sieve to glean the best nuggets from their experience. When they did this, their experience was respected and they became strong leaders. They were able to guide and inspire people around them to learn and grow. They proved to be multipliers.

Then there were those who used their experience as a hammer: "Do what I am asking because I know better from my past experience." Even though they did not use those exact words, that's how it felt to others. They were not effective even if they were right. This lack of humility made it difficult for team members to follow their leadership, even if their ideas were right.

Michael's insight shows us that when experience is used as a hammer, it diminishes team members, regardless of whether the leader was right or wrong. This behavior closes the hearts and minds of your team members, so even if your experience helped you make the right decisions, you may be surprised that those right decisions still led to poor outcomes.

Being curious is a choice. If you have amassed a wonderful body of knowledge with great experience, you still won't go far without a team behind you. Choosing to be curious makes space for others to participate and learn from your experience. While experience might be tempting you to move forward faster, this might only be the right approach for the first sprint of your project. You might go faster by yourself initially, but you will go further with your team.

YOU MIGHT GO FASTER BY YOURSELF INITIALLY, BUT YOU WILL GO FURTHER WITH YOUR TEAM.

I experienced what Michael described when I was a young software applications consultant at Oracle. It was my first job out of school, and I was a sponge. I hated it when a senior consultant directed me on tasks without allowing me to learn and understand what I was tasked to do. And when I asked "Why?" to learn, I would get the answer, "Because I've seen this before, so I'm telling you that this is the right approach!" This was the equivalent of giving me fish to eat instead of teaching me how to fish. I did not learn much working with such senior consultants. I felt demeaned and talked down to.

Be careful not to develop the attitude "You are young and don't understand, so just do what I am asking you to do." Instead, you should choose to be curious about what you can learn from the next generation. Then, ask yourself how you can help bring the younger person along and develop them for future opportunities. If you do that, now you are a multiplier instead of a diminisher and deserve to be a leader.

When we were planning our first customer conference, instead of telling my younger team members how to run the conference, I shared with them my desire to give our customers an unforgettable experience and the chance to build stronger relationships with our company. Then I asked them how they would go about doing that. They surprised me with ideas that I had not thought about before. For example, they suggested providing customers with the opportunity to set up special consulting sessions at the conference to take care of any questions they might have regarding our products. Being curious paid off, and we had a wonderful inaugural customer conference.

If you don't know where to start, leading with a question instead of a directive might help trigger your curiosity.

IDENTIFY AND SOLVE THE RIGHT PROBLEM

After participating in or leading over six hundred strategic planning sessions, I've seen many teams on the verge of solving the wrong problem. When we come together to solve a burning problem, most of the time we are already convinced that we understand the problem well. All we need to do is to discuss, debate, and decide on the best solution. But what if we are not asking the right questions? What if we are really solving the *wrong* problem? Before jumping to find solutions, first ask, "What do we not yet know about this problem? What questions should we be asking?" Pause and choose to be curious.

Ratmir Timashev is a co-founder of Veeam Software and was the CEO until the company passed a billion dollars of revenue and was sold for $5 billion in 2020. We introduced this Rhythm Of Work™ to him after Veeam passed a hundred million in revenues. Ratmir adopted the practice of bringing his execution team together every quarter to discuss key topics. He would listen intently and ask questions. He often wondered out loud if we were answering the right question. This would cause the team to pause and ask, "What do you mean?", providing an opportunity for curiosity to enter the room. When curiosity enters the room, it helps us to zoom out and see the bigger picture.

MICHAEL'S PERSPECTIVE

I've kept this practice, Patrick's Rhythm of Work, since the beginning of AvidXchange. Over twenty-four years, I've had almost one hundred quarterly planning sessions (ninety-four at the writing of this book). It is just too expensive for the team to be led down the wrong path by solving the wrong problems. I maintain this same discipline to pull the team away from their day-to-day work once a quarter to discuss and explore familiar topics, because things change. The problem might have changed while we were heads-down working on it. It is important to slow down in these meetings to ask what we might not yet know and to question if something has changed that might invalidate what we are working on even before we release the solution.

Inertia and past investments make it very difficult to recognize or change our perspective on a topic. That's why being curious helps. Being curious interrupts our existing workflow. Asking what we might not yet know about this topic or what is new about this topic interrupts our flow of work and helps us to see changes and make adjustments.

I'm a very curious person. But even I need someone else facilitating my sessions to help inject more curiosity. It's really a no-brainer when I compare the cost of a professional coach facilitating our session with the cost of my executive team being taken out of the field. The cost of chasing the wrong rabbit or solving the wrong problem is huge. If the facilitator can disrupt our thinking and help us to avoid even one wrong decision, they would have saved us millions in time and resources. So either the leader needs to be a really curious person or they need to have an external facilitator make sure they ask enough questions to solve the right problems.

REPLACE FEAR WITH CURIOSITY

Dr. Stephen Vogt was the founder and CEO of BioPlus, a specialty pharmaceutical company. I met Dr. Vogt in 2012 when BioPlus boasted $126 million in sales and had the privilege of serving him for ten years. As BioPlus grew past $250 million as part of their five-year plan to reach $1 billion in sales, Dr. Vogt was concerned that he might not have the right people in the right seats for the coming years. His team was doing very well at that time, but he was worried about the future. It wasn't just the company's future that bothered him but whether every leader on his team would be able to flourish as the company grew. He was concerned that working on the right organization for BioPlus' future might force him to replace certain leaders who had been integral to bringing the company to its current level of success.

THE FEAR OF THE UNKNOWN SOMETIMES STOPS US FROM EXPLORING POSSIBILITIES. THE IRONY IS THAT EXPLORING POSSIBILITIES OFTEN CREATES MORE OPPORTUNITIES AND OPTIONS.

"Don't be scared," I suggested. "Instead, be curious. Because curiosity touches a lot of things, from innovation to acquisition to customers, as well as culture and mindsets. By replacing fear with curiosity, you might actually develop an exciting future for both BioPlus and your existing leaders." The fear of the unknown sometimes stops us from exploring possibilities. The irony is that exploring possibilities often creates more opportunities and options.

I encouraged Dr. Vogt to work with me and do the future organization exercise for BioPlus and his executive team (for more detail on this exercise, read the chapter "Build a Strong People Ecosystem"). This is a way of building the right organization to give a company its best chance of fulfilling its great destiny while also intentionally developing leaders so that they can flourish as a company grows. Dr. Vogt began by sitting down with each of his executives to discuss what the right role for them might be a year or two ahead. This helped him identify skills gaps and growth opportunities, so the executives had time to develop and would become excited about the future. It not only helped to find the gaps where new hiring might be necessary but also revealed that many of his executives had multiple possibilities for their future roles.

The key to this was Dr. Vogt's curiosity about his people. As he became more curious, he also became more excited about what they might accomplish if they explored the possibilities of the future with him. If they could place their egos aside, understand their strengths, and map those strengths to new opportunities, they might just grow and flourish as the company grew. Armed with curiosity, he approached the process with a positive mindset and a determination to help his executives to flourish.

As a leader, Dr. Vogt impressed me with his interest in learning and leveling up to ensure his company did not outgrow him. He was not exempt from this exercise and recognized that after leading BioPlus for thirty-two years, it was time for some succession planning. He recruited Mark Montgomery to be president of the company and then to take over as CEO in 2021. Sadly, just after completing this transition, Dr. Vogt was diagnosed with brain cancer in late 2021 and passed away the following April.

His curiosity and positivity created a lasting legacy at his company. He created a succession and transition plan without realizing that it would be needed faster than we all desired. Dr. Vogt was a caring and inspiring leader who changed his industry. I am very grateful for the privilege of having been a part of his life and journey.

BOTTOM LINE

1. Curiosity is a choice. Choose to be curious.
2. BE Curious—don't DO Curious.
3. Get interested in what others have to say. This makes you a better listener and a better learner.
4. Don't try to become a better listener. Fix this at the root cause. Focus on being curious.
5. Bonus outcome: Listening shows that you are interested. Being a better listener also helps you build better relationships.
6. People quit people, not companies. Asking the right questions and learning how to care more about your team members will make you a better boss and help you retain your best talent.
7. Hire for curiosity in addition to experience. Experience without curiosity will feel like a hammer and produce bad outcomes.
8. Use curiosity as a filter to determine when to deploy golden nuggets from past experiences rather than using experience as a hammer.
9. Pause and be curious to identify and solve the right problems instead of wasting time on the wrong ones.
10. When you are afraid to engage in tough topics, relax and allow curiosity to help you lean in. Replace fear with curiosity.

CHAPTER 6

LEVEL UP

"If you're not willing to learn, no one can help you. If you're determined to learn, no one can stop you."

–ZIG ZIGLAR

THE STARTUP JOURNEY

Michael and I were laughing at the following illustration.

Mount Startup

This picture says it all!

"Isn't this what happens to us entrepreneurs? Isn't this how we all feel?" Michael explained. "As soon as we declare victory, the next challenge appears. We get to celebrate our victory and then attack the next peak. This is what makes business exciting for me. I love the new challenges that come with the game of business," he said, "and I love improving myself to make the next climb."

"Yes," I agreed. "You solve the problem and press on. But if you can't solve the problem, and get stuck on Mount Growth, your competition passes you by. This is why we all have to constantly learn and grow. We have to level up so that we can play, win, and summit the next peak!"

What if you could proactively level up your knowledge and skill to smooth out your journey? Make it more predictable and sustainable? What if you could replace those cliff-hanging and often existential risky moments with a more predictable journey?

A More Predictable and Sustainable Journey

Many startups do not survive the cliffs, valleys, and peaks that Michael and AvidXchange survived. Those that survive tend to take on a more predictable and sustainable journey. The faster you level up, the better your chances are of surviving the startup phase.

Mount Startup as illustrated in the first figure is also not a mandatory journey. Many serial entrepreneurs who have learned to level up as a consistent habit have been able to enjoy a more enjoyable and predictable startup journey.

Today, AvidXchange is a public company rewarding shareholders with predictable and sustainable performance. Michael has made leveling up part of his everyday journey of running AvidXchange.

THE POWER OF LEVELING UP

Michael derives true delight from improving himself. He loves to find ways to level up! Over the last twenty-four years, Michael has taken all feedback, no matter how tough, as part of the reward of being on his company-building journey.

Michael realizes that he needs to solve the problems of today and simultaneously prepare himself for the challenges of tomorrow. "Patrick, if my company is growing at 30 percent, then I must grow at the same rate or faster, or my company will outgrow me."

IF MY COMPANY IS GROWING AT 30 PERCENT, THEN I MUST GROW AT THE SAME RATE OR FASTER, OR MY COMPANY WILL OUTGROW ME.

AvidXchange is Michael's fourth startup. His journey over thirty years and four startups is a demonstration of repeatedly upskilling to play the game of business at the next level. I recall a coaching session that we had after he'd received some very tough feedback from his board. I asked him how he was doing, and he said he was "fine." I wasn't convinced.

"How can you be 'fine'? That was a very tough session. There's no need to bottle things up. If you're hurting or angry, you need to let that emotion out. I'm your coach. That's what I am here for," I told him.

Michael shared, "One of my board members taught me something previously. He said, 'Bad news is actually *good* news. Because when you receive bad news, you know what you can work on and do something about it.' The board shared with me that I am not currently a CEO who is ready to run a public company. Then they shared with me clearly what it would take for me to fill the gaps and be ready to be that kind of CEO. They showed me what I did not know and made it clear what I need to work on. That is great news, because now I know exactly what I need to do to make myself and AvidXchange successful. How great is that?"

BAD NEWS IS ACTUALLY GOOD NEWS. WHEN YOU RECEIVE BAD NEWS, YOU KNOW WHAT YOU CAN WORK ON AND DO SOMETHING ABOUT IT.

Michael appreciated how his board communicated. He explained that while it is hard to receive feedback, it is also very hard for anyone to deliver feedback, especially if they need to be critical. "So when they do give me critical feedback, it is really a gift. Regardless of whether I agree with the feedback, I receive the gift and say 'thank you.' Then it is really up to me to think about their advice and suggestions. No one is forcing me to apply their insights—that's my choice. They are just giving me feedback and ideas. I have the power and responsibility to decide what I want to do."

"Since you're an NFL guy," he said to me, "I'll go there for my example. The Super Bowl isn't won during that one game. It's won during thousands of hours on the practice field. Since I grew up playing basketball, I have learned to really enjoy training and practice. The practice field is where I work on myself so I'm better able to improve what my coach has identified as my weaknesses. The real problem," he continued, "is when I don't know what to work on, when I can't see what's wrong or how to improve myself. If someone takes the time to show me what I need to work on, that bad news is actually really good news."

"I've got a position on the team," he said, continuing the metaphor, "but it's not quarterback or wide receiver. It's CEO. So, on the practice field, I'm working to be the best CEO I can for my team. When I know what I need to improve, I'm excited to hit the gym and start training. I want my team to win! I want that thrill. And that means I need to be stronger in my position." This lines up with one of AvidXchange's core values: "Win as a Team."

LEVELING UP IN PRACTICE

If you are a leader, your company or team will be limited by your leadership capabilities. If you get stuck on Mount Startup, your whole team will be stuck at the same spot.

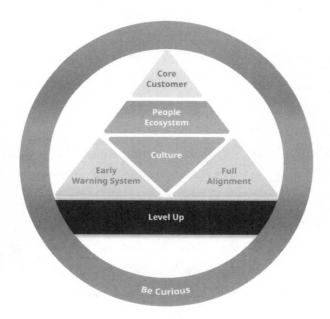

Leveling up is the foundation for continued and repeated success. Michael made the point that we must grow at the same rate or faster than our company's growth or we will become irrelevant and be replaced. Leveling up will allow us to be ready for the next stage of our company's journey. If we as leaders cannot do that, our companies will stagnate, or if we have outside investors, they will replace us.

I was observing my daughter play a video game when it hit me that winning the game of business is similar. When she finished a challenge, her avatar moved on to the next level. At the next level, things moved faster, and her reaction time had to keep pace. The game got harder and more interesting. Some of the monsters were new, and many were the same but bigger. The enemies came harder and faster, and damage to her health points came quicker and was more deadly. She had to learn to move and react much faster, picking up new weapons and skills. She also had to kill the same enemies that she had already learned to kill but with less time and often while solving a different problem simultaneously.

The overall rules were the same: kill the enemies, survive long enough to figure out this level, and then finish it so that she could proceed to the next one. She had to level up by learning new skills, acquiring new weapons, and replenishing her health points faster before hitting zero. She also had to depend on her team to do the same. And when her health points ran out—game over!

Her reward for winning every level was entrance into the next level, where the game again leveled up. Once again, her survival depended on her (and her team) leveling up their skills to win at the new level.

Winning the game of business is very similar. As the business grows to the next level, you will need to solve some of the same problems, but on a larger scale, and the cost of reacting too slowly also increases significantly. You will also meet new challenges that you have never seen before. You need to be aware that even though you are meeting some of the same challenges, you might have to solve them differently as you have less time and new tools at your disposal. The tools and processes that you used in the previous level might be too slow for this level. What got you here might not get you through the next level.

Therefore, leveling up is not a onetime exercise. It needs to happen repeatedly, even continuously.

To do that, you need the right habits. This chapter will share five habits you need to intentionally and consistently develop to level up:

- Habit 1: Delegate to Level Up
- Habit 2: Reflect Regularly to Build Self-Awareness
- Habit 3: Seek and Diffuse Blind Spots
- Habit 4: Learn to Ask for and Receive Feedback
- Habit 5: Work with a Coach

You must level up if you want to succeed. In his book *The 21 Irrefutable Laws of Leadership*, John Maxwell writes about the Law of the Lid. He shares that leadership ability determines the effectiveness and potential of a leader. He shares the story of how Dick and Maurice McDonald's leadership abilities allowed them to have initial success with McDonald's. But it was not until they brought in Ray Kroc, a man with a much higher leadership ability, that McDonald's scaled up to the powerhouse franchise that we all know today.

Leveling up is not an option; it is mandatory. If you do not level up, your company will stagnate. You will be the limiting factor, the reason why your company fails. This is true about all leaders at your company. If they do not level up, their departments will stagnate and your best employees will leave.

WHAT PREVENTS YOU FROM LEVELING UP

Dealing with the Urgent

I came home exhausted from a very grueling week. My wife, Pei-Yee, mentioned how tired I looked and how hard I must have worked during the week. She then asked me what I had accomplished that week. I paused, thought about it, but could not answer her. I realized that I had worked very hard but not in an intentional way. I had a lot of meetings, ran to help solve one problem after the other, but in the grand scheme of things, I could not answer the simple question "What did I actually accomplish this week?" That's a bad week. That's a week where I was ruled by the tyranny of the urgent and did not prioritize what I would choose to get done. I got all kinds of things done but none of my top priorities. If you don't rule your work, your work will rule you.

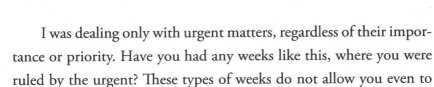

IF YOU DON'T RULE YOUR WORK, YOUR WORK WILL RULE YOU.

I was dealing only with urgent matters, regardless of their importance or priority. Have you had any weeks like this, where you were ruled by the urgent? These types of weeks do not allow you even to *think* about leveling up, let alone prioritizing any activities to improve yourself. And if you string too many urgent weeks together, there is a good chance you will miss something really important.

Most activities that help you to level up tend to fall into the "important but not urgent" category. They prepare you for the challenges of tomorrow. Of course, some urgent matters, especially the existential ones, will force you to level up. Standing atop one peak, staring at the cliff you must navigate to reach the next peak, represents such existential leveling up opportunities. If you level up, you survive, and if you do not, you die. These challenges also generate a lot of waste as you have to jump off the cliff and resume climbing at a lower elevation to get to the next peak. This represents waste and rework.

Not Prioritizing Tomorrow

Working as a leader in a growth company already presents many challenging opportunities to solve for today. It is really hard to prioritize tomorrow. Prioritizing for tomorrow means choosing to take energy away from the urgency of today and intentionally channeling that time and energy toward the near future.

Ratmir Timashev is a co-founder and former CEO of Veeam. We met when Ratmir was proactively looking for tools to help Veeam continue their growth journey from a hundred million in revenue to a billion. His proactive search led him to us.

When I reviewed Veeam, I was impressed by how well they were executing their strategy. Their financial results also reflected their excellent execution. I asked Ratmir what he needed and how we could serve him.

He shared that Veeam was his second venture. He had already led a very successful startup and sold his first company to Microsoft. As Veeam was already over a hundred million in revenues and still growing at a fast rate, he knew from experience that he needed help. He needed a simple way or framework to continue his climb. This time, he was planning to have a different journey up Mount Startup.

"You have to have the self-belief to quit your job, and to be certain you're making something so cool that others will also quit their jobs to come and join you. At the same time," he added, "you need to be humble enough to admit when you need help." He recalled our meeting from ten years ago. "I needed some guidance. I needed to know: What do you see that I don't see?" He wanted someone from the outside to provide additional insights and patterns that would help him. "I'm not very ego-driven," he said, "I'm always analyzing myself. For me, growth, curiosity, and awareness are all part of the same thing."

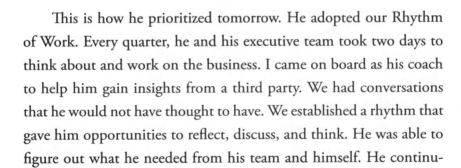

THIS IS HOW HE PRIORITIZED TOMORROW. HE ADOPTED OUR RHYTHM OF WORK. EVERY QUARTER, HE AND HIS EXECUTIVE TEAM TOOK TWO DAYS TO THINK ABOUT AND WORK ON THE BUSINESS.

This is how he prioritized tomorrow. He adopted our Rhythm of Work. Every quarter, he and his executive team took two days to think about and work on the business. I came on board as his coach to help him gain insights from a third party. We had conversations that he would not have thought to have. We established a rhythm that gave him opportunities to reflect, discuss, and think. He was able to figure out what he needed from his team and himself. He continuously leveled up as he guided Veeam to over a billion in revenue and a very successful exit.

Not Investing in Your Own Growth and Learning

Early in my entrepreneur journey, I felt guilty when I spent money for my own learning. I was young and believed I should invest in my employees before I invested in myself. During a negotiation for a large contract with a Fortune 500 company, I was experiencing various negotiation tactics that bullied me into a sense of helplessness and foreboding. I knew I was out of my depth. We were small, and it felt like a life-or-death negotiation. I had reached an "Oh Shit!" peak.

Then, a one-page course description on negotiation came across my desk: "Getting to Yes and Dealing with Difficult People" by Roger Fisher and Willian Ury at Harvard University. It was exactly what I needed to learn. I felt as though God had just answered my prayers. Bam! I am in!

It was an expensive class. I found myself negotiating with myself to invest in this class. "It's only money. I have to do this or I will die at the hands of this professional negotiator!" The course was excellent. It opened my eyes to many things. I learned that negotiation, like other skills, could be learned. I wasn't a bad negotiator, as I'd feared—just an untrained one. As I worked through the modules, I began to see the range of tactics my would-be client had used and then to see through them. I'd allowed myself to become scared and intimidated, wrapped up in the fear of losing this lucrative deal. But now that I'd educated myself, I was able to confidently counter them and work on win-win deals. I had leveled up.

LEADERS SHOULD LEARN FIRST, AND THEN THEY CAN COACH AND GUIDE WITH KNOWLEDGE.

In hindsight, I was really fortunate I had reached this life-or-death negotiation. I did not know what I did not know. I did not know that win-win negotiation was a gap in my skill set. I did not know what a win-win deal looked like. This Harvard negotiation class leveled me up. It changed my paradigm on negotiation forever and equipped me with the right skills to negotiate win-win deals. Without that, I would have negotiated a win-lose deal that might have killed my company.

Leaders should always be learning; they'll be better equipped with knowledge to coach and guide. I learned not to feel guilty about investing in improving myself. I learned that my company deserved the best CEO I could possibly be. And yours does too. Invest in yourself, level up, and be the CEO that your company needs and deserves.

Ego and Lack of Self-Awareness

Questions advance your learning as you level up in any area. To learn, we need to be curious and ask questions. All of us must let go of any ideas or mental barriers that hinder asking questions.

When you were a child, born with curiosity, you had no problems asking questions. You did not differentiate between smart and stupid questions. They were just questions. Then you grew up and your ego developed. Now you might have thoughts floating in your mind that hinder your growth and learning. You might think, "If I ask that question, they might think I am incompetent," or, "I should already know this. Why don't I know this?"

These are all variations on the same theme of your ego hindering your curiosity to learn. There are no bad questions or good questions. There are only questions. Questions also help us make less assumptions. The wrong assumptions can cost you your job.

Bob Potter was the CEO at SentryOne when they successfully completed their journey and sold the company to SolarWinds. Long before SentryOne, he had his first CEO opportunity at Kalido. He'd guided this London-based data management software company from $5.5 million in sales to over $20 million in under three years. "I thought I was the cat's meow, that I couldn't possibly fail," he told me. He was promoted to CEO. Young and ego-driven, he made assumptions and was not curious enough to listen to advisors.

He was organizing the C-round, a third round of investment in the company, and had a specific aim. "I thought my job was to raise money at the highest possible valuation. If I could have gotten $100 million, I'd have done it. It turned out that I was wrong. My ego wanted the highest valuation possible, but my lead investor wanted a more realistic valuation that protected them from being crammed down by a future investment round. I lacked self-awareness and was not listening to their needs and their experience. The knives came out and I was done!"

The investors replaced Bob and told him that he had failed as a CEO. They taught him that his role was to raise capital for the company and not to muscle in on the investors by insisting on determining the company's valuation. "It was a humbling lesson about ego," he remembers, "and about the dangers of being stubborn. I'd fallen in love with an idea of how to do something instead of seeking to learn the best way to get that done."

Years later, as CEO of SentryOne, his investors asked for a 360-degree review of his leadership. He took the feedback seriously. "I read the report," he said, "and found things I really needed to work on. The best CEOs have humility. They know they must get better. The ones who are all about themselves and their ego are not as good as they think they are."

"Ego needs good judgment," Bob mused. "You do need a strong ego and drive to be a successful CEO. You do need to have confidence and self-belief. But you also need to temper that with curiosity and humility. If you take yourself too seriously, you will stifle good people around you, and you will inadvertently kill great ideas."

So now, Bob listens more than he talks. "I go to every meeting I can. Mostly I sit there and listen without talking. Sometimes I ask questions to elicit views, opinions, and some background about people. It's like a learned behavior."

"I believe you can become self-aware, and you must commit to getting better," Bob continued. "I used to think that I'm better than I actually am, and my ego wanted to show what I know. But I learned, as I got older, that I can and must improve. That's why I hired a coach. Having a coach who has the ability to see what I can't see has helped me get stronger even more quickly. It is not something that I could have done by myself, even if I worked harder."

Bob's coach helped him see past his ego and even helped him recognize his blind spots and learn how to protect himself against those. Freeing himself from ego and gaining self-awareness helped Bob to level up.

HABITS TO LEVEL UP

Leveling up does not happen automatically or by chance. It is hard work. If you wish to be successful, you can't expect to level up just once or occasionally. You need to level up repeatedly. That's why you need the right habits.

Habit 1: Delegate to Level Up

Serial entrepreneur Colin C. Campbell (author of *Start. Scale. Exit. Repeat.*) shared his research with me: "Ninety-nine percent of US businesses are 'small.' They were destined to be that way. It's because their leaders fail to scale." He links this failure with bad CEO habits:

they allow themselves to become the limiting factor, the reason why growth is strangled. "A common limiting factor comes from CEOs who can't let go of responsibilities," Colin told me. "They have not learned how to let others take on leadership roles, run their divisions and be responsible for them."

Colin shares how delegation changes as the company grows. "Delegation is a good example. As a company grows and matures, leaders also need to grow and mature in how they delegate. Initially, it's about delegating tasks to individuals when you are in startup mode. But when you reach scale mode, you need to learn how to delegate responsibilities, not just tasks. This is very different. It's a real mindset shift."

MICHAEL'S PERSPECTIVE

I agree with Colin. I have had to learn how to level up the way I delegate work. It is a different skill and process to delegate responsibilities instead of tasks. It is common knowledge that as the company gets larger, we need to learn how to delegate more. Generic advice to "delegate more" is common knowledge yet not specific enough to be helpful.

IF YOU CAN'T SEE IT, YOU PROBABLY CAN'T DO IT.

In order to delegate responsibilities, I have asked team members to visualize what success looks like. Patrick often reminds me that if you can't see it, then you probably can't do it. I keep this in mind and ask more questions to help my team members visualize and articulate what success looks like. If they can describe success, it also gives me the confidence to believe that they can get it done. Once that happens, I can trust them to achieve their responsibilities. And when I can trust them to succeed, that's when I feel confident to let go and delegate the responsibility of achieving the overall goal or department. I've had to learn this. It took time, observation, and my coach to point it out and for me to be more self-aware and practice delegating differently.

This also applies to all the leaders who work for AvidXchange. Leveling up is not just for CEOs—it is for all leaders. If a leader does not level up, this blocks the growth of their team and department. Such leaders will unintentionally hold back our company from achieving our goals.

Habit 2: Reflect Regularly to Build Self-Awareness

The best leaders are self-aware. Many gurus have written about this premise, so I will rely on their work. Daniel Goleman wrote in his book *Emotional Intelligence* (EI) that self-awareness is one of the four domains in his EI model and that EI is critical for leaders to be effective with their team members.

So let's work on how to become more self-aware. Growing self-awareness is a journey that we are all already on. Even if you do not do anything intentional, you naturally will notice things about yourself as time passes. However, you can accelerate your progress significantly by being intentional about regular self-reflection. Self-reflection is also a familiar practice. Most of us reflect when special moments happen. When something really wonderful happens, you may think, "Wow. How did that happen? How do I do that again?" Now you are more self-aware and might try to repeat that victory. When something painful happens, your thought may be, "Dude, that was terrible. How did I walk into that? Don't do that again!" Now you will consciously avoid activities that you believe might bring about that negative outcome. These moments are rocks of wisdom that fell on you hard enough, so you noticed, reflected, and learned. Each time this happens, you get a little more self-aware.

You already know how to reflect because you do it during life's biggest moments. You can build on your success by creating a routine of regular reflection. Discover the small stuff. There are tiny grains of wisdom falling around you daily that you might not notice. You need a way to notice them, or you will miss them. A habit or regular routine of self-reflection will help you to see and collect these grains of wisdom.

Put This Habit of Self-Reflection into Your Flight Path

The initial response I usually receive when I suggest regular reflection and journaling is an easy "Yes." It makes sense. So why not? Over the years, I have seen many leaders jump into this with enthusiasm only to report back that they were unable to accomplish what at first appeared to be an easy task. After guiding leaders through their initial failure, I realized a pattern. This is so simple to do that many were deceived by its simplicity—they did not realize that simple is not the same as easy! They thought it would just happen when they decided to start this process.

NEWS FLASH: SIMPLE DOES NOT MEAN EASY.

One common mistake is deciding to do this first thing in the morning without realizing how this will change your morning routine. This often means that you have to make the decision to wake up thirty minutes earlier. Somehow the alarm clock does not get the memo, and you find yourself in your regular morning routine without any time built in for reflection. Then the week ends, and you did not reflect. And discouragement begins to set in.

Here are some simple tips to get you started:

- Start by self-reflecting once a week.
- Choose a time that fits your schedule well, when there is natural downtime.
- Don't try harder—try differently. If you fail, be kind to yourself, and find a different or better time.

DON'T TRY HARDER—TRY DIFFERENTLY.

If you fail initially, recognize that the culprit is not you. Rather, it's your process. Don't get discouraged. Fix the process. Find an easy way to slip this into your regular routine. Don't make it any harder on yourself.

Start slow, with low expectations for yourself, and build momentum. Once you have mastered the habit of weekly self-reflection, consider adding a midweek reflection. When you are successful with that, consider moving your reflection to a daily routine. You don't have to. If you are able to create a habit of self-reflection once a week and keep that habit going, congratulations! You are already very successful.

Look for positive things to reflect on. Most of us naturally choose events that did not go well to drive our self-reflection. Make sure you intentionally reflect on victories as well.

Templates for Self-Reflection

Here are some templates to help you get started.

Template 1: Reflection to Learn and Move Forward

This is a simple template designed to help you learn about yourself to improve your self-awareness and prioritization skills. Start with this, and customize it for your own needs as you get more comfortable with the habit of self-reflection.

1. Start with gratitude. Who are three people, or what are three things that I am thankful for?
2. What are three events that happened this week that I can learn from?
   - Something positive? A victory that I would like to repeat?
   - Something I missed?
3. What are three priorities that I will accomplish next week?
   - Pull up your goals for the quarter and consider them.
   - Pull up your calendar and review your commitments.
   - Schedule time to accomplish these three priorities.

Great weeks do not happen by chance. They happen intentionally. I suggest setting aside thirty minutes for this template, ten minutes for each of the three sections. Reflect weekly at a minimum. Each year provides you with fifty-two weeks to learn and move forward stronger and with more confidence.

During the week, celebrate when you achieve the three priorities that you committed to achieve. Pat yourself on the back a little. This is especially important if you are a CEO. CEOs have the biggest jobs with the least amount of regular appreciation and recognition. Take the opportunity to tell yourself that you did a good job.

If you would like to learn and get more self-aware quicker, then turn this self-reflection flywheel faster! Do this daily instead of weekly. Some of the leaders I work with practice this self-reflection habit daily. This gives them 365 opportunities a year to learn and level up instead of 52!

Template 2: Developing My Self-Awareness and Leadership

This template is designed to help you reflect and learn how to improve your emotional intelligence. What is the effect you have on the people you lead? Do you inspire and motivate? Or do you unintentionally diminish the people around you?

1. My energy: Where did it go this week?
   - What energized me?
   - What sucked the life out of me?
2. My team: How did they work with me?
   - Positive: What did they like about working with me this week?
   - Negative: What did they not like about working with me this week?
3. My language: What impact did my words have on my team?
   - Did I have an opportunity to praise anyone? How did I do that?
   - Did I have an opportunity to coach or correct anyone? How did I do that?

Habit 3: Seek and Diffuse Blind Spots

Blind spots in cars make it easier for accidents to happen. Today, most new cars have blind spot warning indicators to warn you that a car is in that area that is not made visible by your mirrors. In the old days, before these indicators were common on cars, I almost had an accident. I checked my mirrors, and seeing no cars, I signaled and moved into the right lane rather decisively. Suddenly, a car appeared out of nowhere, blasted their horn, stomped on their brakes, and narrowly avoided a collision with me!

I am thankful for my blind spot warning indicator. When it lights up, I do not think, "Why the heck would that thing light up? There's nothing there!" Even though I don't see the car in my mirrors, I believe that it is helping me avoid an accident.

Leaders have blind spots. Accidents happen. Unlike car collisions, business accidents cause damage that we do not hear or see, unless someone is kind enough to tell us. As part of your process of leveling up, you must seek out your blind spots. Blind spots stop your progress. By definition, they are invisible to you. You can't improve that area of yourself because you can't see the issues; therefore, it won't occur to you to learn more about your blind spots. Other people will be slow to mention these blind spots to you because they are concerned that you will receive such feedback negatively. If you want to learn more, you have to intentionally seek your blind spots out. You also need to develop a thicker skin and be ready to hear what might surprise you. When you, the student, are ready, the teacher appears!

WHEN YOU, THE STUDENT, ARE READY, THE TEACHER APPEARS!

Amy Ankrum was promoted to be the CEO of Qualtrax, a compliance software company that primarily serves heavily regulated industries. I asked her how she leveled up to take on this role and continued to level up repeatedly to succeed. Amy shared that it takes a very humble person to be willing to hear about their blind spots. Since she was not the founder of Qualtrax and did not have a software background, she came into the role believing that she had a lot to learn. She sought out experienced CEOs to help her learn faster. She was grateful and surprised how gracious these experienced CEOs were to help her. "One of the things that was brought to light was that I should get an executive coach, and that was one of the first things I did. I spent a lot of time working with that individual on my blind spots."

"I can have strong opinions and get very excited or passionate about things I believe we should do. That can come across like I have already made up my mind, and I am not going to hear the other ideas. But in my mind, I am thinking the opposite. I am so excited to hear and explore what we are going to try. This is one area that I found very important. I had my coach also coach my executive team in this area."

When her coach discovered some of her blind spots and brought them to her attention, she was surprised. She thought they had a very open culture and wondered why her people did not volunteer these insights earlier. She shared, "But at the end of the day, it was a gift that my coach was able to draw out, and it did change the way I interacted with my team."

Qualtrax was successful because Amy realized that it was important for her to level up. She invested in a coach and also invested in her executive team. "I committed to my one-on-ones. I think this is something that I have seen some leaders sacrifice too quickly. This was precious time. It was my team members' time to get on the table anything that they needed to. I always asked them what I could be doing for them. This was another way to check for blind spots. As a leader you have got to really read the room. Be careful not to shut people down. It really kills innovation."

MICHAEL'S PERSPECTIVE

Blind spots are an area that I am constantly working on. Even after you discover your blind spots, it is so easy to fall back into those practices when time is short and you have critical deliverables in front of you. Like Amy, I have invited my executive team members to call out my blind spots, but it is hard for them, and it's not natural. It's more natural to get such feedback from a seasoned coach who has the right patterns in their experience. I work very closely with my board, and they are not shy about letting me know what blind spots I need to work on. I truly am thankful for that. It is really a gift to have people around me who help me see and grow.

Every day at AvidXchange, I am running the biggest company I have ever run. It is fun and exciting. So every day when I get up, I'd better be learning and finding ways to level up if I want us to continue our journey of growth and success.

Habit 4: Learn to Ask for and Receive Feedback

Dr. Jay Cohen recalled how his staffing company, Signature Consultants, had quickly grown to about $50 million. A physician by training, Jay had found a happy marriage of his two great focuses in life: technology and compassion. The same pairing of interests that had underpinned his interest in medicine now fueled his business, a "heart-first" recruitment firm that was setting itself apart.

Even as they were successful and growing, his business partner, Geoff Gray, was trying to help Jay see unmet needs. Geoff gave Jay some tough feedback. "Geoff was dissatisfied with my organizational side. He was super well organized, and so was my COO, but I really wasn't. How's that for self-awareness?" Jay laughed. He knew that his own approach wasn't going to properly support the growth of a firm that had real potential to reach the next level. "I knew I was going to have to reinvent myself periodically as the company grew," he said. "Or hire someone. Or get out of the way. Or sell it."

The key was honest feedback from his colleagues. "We were in it together, so no matter how well we were doing, we weren't going to rest on our laurels. You can always do better. I had people who were looking at the stuff I was doing, and they were telling me what they thought—nicely," he clarifies, "and with kindness. Because they cared about me. We espoused a philosophy: 'Friends don't let friends drive drunk.' If someone was making a mistake, you had to tell them. That's an obligation."

Jay made it as easy as possible for people around him to give him feedback. Just as it is hard to give someone honest and critical feedback, it is also hard to receive it yourself. If you receive feedback poorly, your reaction will discourage others from giving you feedback.

IF YOU RECEIVE FEEDBACK POORLY, YOUR REACTION WILL DISCOURAGE OTHERS FROM GIVING YOU FEEDBACK.

Regardless of whether or not you found the feedback useful, know that it took courage for someone to provide you with feedback. The person also cares about your success enough to take a risk and share their observations. To encourage feedback for yourself, I suggest you receive feedback with a "Thank you" regardless of what you thought about it. You can thank the person for caring about you enough to take a risk and share their thoughts with you. You can ponder that feedback, and in your self-reflection time, take the time to consider if you can see what they see.

Be careful not to debate or explain why the situation happened. As soon as you try to explain it, the other person will perceive it as you becoming defensive and feel awkward. This feeling of unease might cause them to stop providing feedback in the future. After all, they just gave you a gift, and they were not expecting to learn more or debate the situation with you. Be careful to say "Thank you," smile, and process it later.

Habit 5: Work with a Coach

Both Jay Cohen and Amy Ankrum leveled up faster and achieved better outcomes with their companies by working with coaches. As well as being remarkably self-aware, Jay was also generous in his appreciation for those who'd helped him through the years, especially his coaches. "I would never have achieved what I did without their help," he said. "It's worth remembering," he added, "there's no extra credit for doing it yourself."

The best athletes have coaches. In fact, many of them have multiple coaches to help them make progress in all areas of their sport. The best coaches are able to observe you and help you to consider growth opportunities from patterns that they recognize.

In the NFL, we see that quarterbacks who get traded to a new team perform differently under different coaches with different systems. Their success is not only dependent on their skill and ability. It is also highly dependent on the system they are in and the ability of their coaches to get the most out of their skill. When you look for a coach, consider the following:

- Patterns: Patterns are analogous to a coach's system. Think about what patterns you need to learn and grow.
- Chemistry: You need to be able to be vulnerable with your coach and share the good, the bad, and the ugly.
- Time: Review your coaching relationship every year. You might need a different coach after a few years to help you as you level up, and your company faces new and different opportunities and challenges.

MICHAEL'S PERSPECTIVE

I have been very lucky. I have worked with coaches who truly put AvidXchange first before their own interests. Patrick even pushed me toward a different coach when he believed I needed someone different for that stage of our growth.

I also have different coaches for different purposes:

- My CEO Coach helps me with the big picture of executing our strategy.
- My Leadership Coach helps us with becoming better leaders at each stage of our growth.
- My Speaker Coach helps prepare me for speaking events.
- My Tennis Coach helps me continue to improve my tennis game.

BOTTOM LINE

1. Check if you fall prey to any of these inhibitors, and take action to change:

   □ not prioritizing and making time to learn and level up,

   □ not investing in your own growth and filling your own gaps as a leader, and

   □ ego and lack of self-awareness.

2. Leveling up requires habit building—it's continuous, not a single event.

3. Put self-reflection into your flight path to make it easier to create and do this habit.

4. Seek and diffuse blind spots.

5. Become an expert at asking and receiving feedback.

6. When you receive feedback, say "Thank you," and process the information later.

7. Find and work with the right coaches. If you do not think you need a coach, it might be because you have not actively searched for the right person to join you in your journey.

CHAPTER 7

ESTABLISH YOUR EARLY WARNING SYSTEM

"Risk comes from not knowing what you're doing."

—WARREN BUFFETT

MY FIRST EARLY WARNING SYSTEM

It was 2 a.m. I woke up in a cold sweat with my heart pounding. My gut told me that my company was headed for a train wreck. But how could that be? I had great talent on my team. Clients were happy. Our Key Performance Indicators (KPIs) all looked good. Plus, we spent tons of time on a weekly basis to review project plans and statuses. So how could we be headed for a train wreck?

I tried to dismiss this moment by writing it off to stress. But I was wide awake with adrenaline flowing, so going back to sleep wasn't an option. I had to either validate my instinct and take evasive action or prove to myself that I had nothing to worry about. What could I look at to reassure myself that there was no impending disaster? What could I measure that would allow me to peer just a little into the future in order to avoid being blindsided?

It was 1996, and I was running Metasys, a startup that transformed the way large companies shipped products to their customers while saving them 5–15 percent of their overall transportation budget. Metasys was a rocket ship! Growing at 100 percent each year, we achieved the rank of 151 on the Inc. 500. We were working hard, playing hard, hardly sleeping, and loving it. Our hair was on fire!

Our clients were companies like FedEx, Monsanto, Cisco Systems, and Levi Strauss. They were all Fortune 500 companies with hard, unforgiving deadlines. We had detailed weekly project status meetings that went over complex project plans, deliverables, and deadlines. We spared no expense in hiring top project management talent from some of the best consulting firms. In hindsight, those status meetings seemed laborious, painful, and ineffective.

Maybe we were asking the wrong questions. The project KPIs we were reviewing measured past activities and financial results. KPIs such as "Revenues per Employee" and "Modules Delivered per Team Member" provided an excellent review of past performance. But we weren't getting warnings about possible train wrecks down the line. The night I woke up in a cold sweat, I knew our KPIs were providing answers to the wrong questions. I needed leading indicators that would help us look ahead instead of looking back.

I spent that night coming up with the right questions. These questions were translated into KPIs that provided us with our first forward-looking dashboard, much like how a car's headlights illuminate the road ahead for the driver. Between the hours of 2 a.m. and 8 a.m., I designed a dashboard with three categories containing a total of nine KPIs.

The three categories I chose were Company, Employees, and Customers. Each category had three KPIs. This dashboard included a spreadsheet with weeks across the top so that I could track new data each week and make decisions based on forward-looking indicators.

The next morning I met with my head of consulting, Jack. I asked Jack to inspect our projects according to these KPIs and deliver the results to me by the next morning. Jack was not inspired by this new, non-revenue-generating assignment and insisted that our current weekly status meetings were already doing the job. Since I did not give him a choice, Jack grudgingly agreed to the assignment.

We proceeded to work on how we would measure and report on these KPIs. Jack first worked to refine and confirm the KPIs. The temptation was to add more measurements. I insisted that we could only have three per category. "You can change up the KPIs, but you can only have three!" I believed having more than three KPIs would steal our attention from the most important ones. Each KPI had three specific bands of performance, color coded to Red, Yellow, or Green:

- Green meant that things were good.
- Yellow indicated that we had encountered a difficulty that could be resolved with some advice and help from management.
- Red meant that we were headed toward a train wreck and immediate intervention was needed.

We worked on and agreed to specific criteria on how each KPI should be statused Red, Yellow, or Green. These criteria would clarify expectations and allow Jack to provide a status objectively instead of relying on his gut. After we reached an agreement on Red, Yellow, and

Green criteria for every KPI, Jack was ready to start measuring and providing weekly status updates.

The next Monday, Jack walked in, looking embarrassed. When he showed me his dashboard, I understood why: it was full of Reds and Yellows! We were headed toward multiple train wrecks. My heart-pounding, 2 a.m. instincts were right after all. Jack asked if he still had a job, and I emphatically replied, "Yes! Otherwise, who's going to clean up this mess? Me?"

We agreed that it was important to have a dashboard process that took measurements regularly and consistently. Jack agreed to the following new activities:

1. Take measurements or collect data every Friday, and then publish his dashboard each Monday.
2. Assign a score and rate everything according to the agreed-upon success criteria.
3. Work with his project managers to develop similar project dashboards for every customer project.
4. Display the dashboards publicly on doors and walls.

Jack was initially taken aback by the idea of displaying these dashboards in public, especially since he felt that people would see only Reds and Yellows. These detailed dashboards might embarrass his project managers. Jack pleaded, "Why don't we fix these problems first and then display these dashboards publicly? That way we won't scare or upset other team members." I assured him that embarrassing him or anyone else was not my agenda. My sole intent was to arrive at the best solutions to our problems in the shortest possible time.

If we attempted to fix the problems before displaying the dashboards, we would only have two brains working on these problems: Jack and myself. If we shared the dashboards transparently and asked the whole team for help, we would be able to activate all the brains in the consulting group. The promise of tapping into the power of our collective intelligence provided Jack with the courage to display these dashboards publicly.

SELF-PRESERVATION, FEAR, AND EMBARRASSMENT. THESE THREE POWERFUL FORCES BRING DRAMA INTO A COMPANY.

Jack's initial reaction—fix the problems before making the dashboards public—is very typical. Unfortunately, it stemmed from self-preservation, fear, and embarrassment. These three powerful forces bring drama into a company, and then a lack of candor makes everything worse. Progress slows down, and the focus becomes moderating how things appear to others, not actually solving the issues. This is how drama blinds teams to impending train wrecks. In contrast, dashboards will help you lead without drama to focus on the right issues, collaborating to come up with faster solutions and actions that will avoid train wrecks and ultimately steer you to success.

DRAMA BLINDS TEAMS TO IMPENDING TRAIN WRECKS. IN CONTRAST, DASHBOARDS WILL HELP YOU LEAD WITHOUT DRAMA TO FOCUS ON THE RIGHT ISSUES.

I will never forget what happened the following Monday. The dashboards went up on the walls, and everyone was shocked by the Red and Yellow statuses. That's when the real fun began.

It turned out to be the best thing we could have done. I explained to my team that my objective was neither to berate nor to place blame. The initial dashboard was our baseline. It did not matter how we got to our baseline. Only what we chose to do moving forward truly mattered. I encouraged every single team member to figure out how we could collectively drive our dashboard status from Reds and Yellows to Greens. When I look back now, I can say, "Hey! We chose to focus on the problems, not the people."

By framing the initial dashboards as a baseline to work from and improve, people were not embarrassed by the red KPIs on their dashboards. In fact, it felt like receiving a Get Out of Jail Free card in Monopoly. We all focused on getting the Reds to improve to Greens. A flurry of activity broke out—meetings, discussions, suggestions, and solutions. For the next few months, I did two things consistently. First, I ensured that these dashboards were done and posted publicly by Monday morning without exception—and believe me, there were tons of excuses. They did not have to be complete or ready, but without fail, they went up on the walls. Second, I walked down the hallways, studied them, and brainstormed solutions with many team members. Over the next few months, most of the Red and Yellow KPIs turned to Green.

We survived by avoiding multiple train wrecks with our customers. We had just saved our company by having the right leading indicators. We focused on them and made adjustments weekly, inviting as many brains as we could to solve problems. We focused on solutions instead of blaming the people who brought the problems to light.

WE FOCUSED ON SOLUTIONS INSTEAD OF BLAMING THE PEOPLE WHO BROUGHT THE PROBLEMS TO LIGHT.

This experience showed me five key lessons that we can all apply:

1. Develop an early warning system. Avoid potential issues by using leading indicators that can make predictions and alert you to possible train wrecks. Keep them future focused and predictive.

2. Begin with clear success criteria. Avoid rework and wasted resources. Don't start any projects until you can describe what success looks like using simple Red-Yellow-Green success criteria.

3. Be transparent, and engage all brains available. Share candidly what the real problems are while allowing teammates to engage their abilities to solve the problems.

4. Tackle problems, not people. Keep your team out of the foxhole of self-preservation with a focus on the problem, not whose fault it is.

5. Reward results, not effort. Avoid the common mistake of rewarding long hours and superhuman effort. Reward team members for achieving agreed-upon success criteria, and celebrate achieving stretch goals.

This dashboard became my early warning system. Do you have something similar? It seems simple, yet most CEOs and executives I meet lack an early warning system.

THE POWER OF AN EARLY WARNING SYSTEM

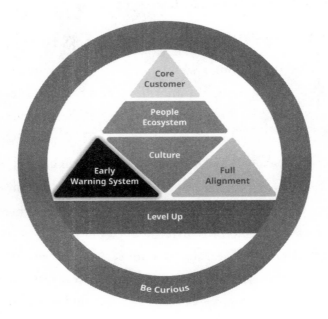

An early warning system saved my first company. Most of us do not think about having one until something goes wrong. Then we wake up and "close the barn door after the horse ran out," finally building our early warning system long after it should have been up and running.

We should all build an early warning system as soon as we can in order to avoid the train wrecks and failures that are waiting for us along our journeys.

EXCUSES THAT PREVENT US FROM BUILDING AN EARLY WARNING SYSTEM

We Don't Have Time

This kind of early warning system is simple but not easy to build. It takes a lot of time to observe, think, and reflect before you can figure out what your early warning system needs to include. It is different for every company and changes according to the challenges and opportunities they are facing. The irony is that urgency is created by crisis. To stop the crisis, you need time to think. Stopping to think takes discipline and commitment. At Metasys, we stopped what we were doing and decided to work differently instead of working harder. "I don't have time" is an age-old excuse. God gave you and I the same amount of time: twenty-four hours in a day. The truth is that it is easier to work harder and scarier to stop, think, and work smarter. It's a choice that I encourage you to make today.

Successful Results

Results are lagging indicators. They are typically measurements of fruits that were already planted, watered, nurtured, and harvested. Results' indicators don't tell you about the next crop of fruit. It is very easy to feel comfortable with the good results you have harvested and not pay attention to the leading indicators that tell you about how the next set of crops are faring. Will your next harvest also be strong, or will you be facing a famine?

A CEO called me recently and shared with me that his company had just finished the year with very strong results. They had both good revenue growth and solid profits. Yet, his gut was signaling that disaster could be around the corner. He asked, "Patrick, given your experience with so many growth companies, what do you think? Are we OK, or do you think we are teetering on the edge of a ditch? I should feel great with the results we just delivered, but I'm worried about the coming year." This CEO was not fooled by his good results. His gut was warning him about things that he did not know how to see. It's a good thing he listened to his gut, as he then built an excellent early warning system of leading indicators.

Believing Your Own Hype

Your public relations and your marketing departments both talk about how great you and your company are. Their job is to serve a particular flavor of Kool-Aid to the world. But it's not for your own consumption. Don't drink your own Kool-Aid by believing in your own press!

Most of the time when a well-known company fails, people who do not know the company intimately are surprised. We say things like, "Wow, I thought they were doing great," or, "How did that happen? They just won a big contract," or, "They just opened ten new stores! How could they have failed?" This is because the observers were reading positive PR and marketing stories. So don't believe your own hype. Besides, even if you were as good as your PR claims you are, why wouldn't you want an early warning system to prevent disasters before they happen?

STORIES OF SUCCESS

MICHAEL'S EXPERIENCE

In 2007, my company, AvidXchange, was doing well. Growing at an annual rate of more than 50 percent, we were showing a lot of promise. But this growing success was happening against the backdrop of one of the worst banking crises we'd ever seen. Investor sentiment was very conservative, and they were in wait-and-see mode, holding on to their cash until it was clear which companies would make it through this crisis.

They had good reasons for caution. With banks failing and the big three automotive companies in Detroit approaching the government for assistance, equity investors were very conservative with their investments. My board asked a good question: "Michael, you are growing and doing well. But you still need to understand that it will be impossible for us to raise capital in the current market. That means you'll need to grow with the capital you have. You must not run out of cash, even if you have to slow your growth."

My board then asked Patrick, "How do we know how much growth AvidXchange can achieve without running out of cash? No matter how good a company AvidXchange is, we can't raise more capital in the current market." He suggested that we build an early warning system that we called our Stop Signs Dashboard. It would have a few of the right leading indicators that would warn us to stop growing and spending money if their status turned to Red.

These were tough questions to grapple with, and I couldn't yet see the answers for myself. Patrick went into learning mode, asking me questions about where our sales were coming from, how they were converted into cash, and how we processed our receivables. He helped me to drill down and figure out how accurate our sales forecasts were. What could we realistically depend on during this likely cash crunch? He asked deeper questions, and I started to hear "Why?" a lot more, followed by, "OK, how do you do that?" We interrogated my business to discover root causes that might adversely affect our cash flow.

After dozens of questions and some intensive discussion, we had a breakthrough. I listed a few simple ways of measuring our current business situation, and these became our new leading indicators. That sounds simple, but it's really hard to do and even harder by yourself. Working with a coach like Patrick was critical to figuring out the right leading indicators.

We looked at a number of metrics:

- Our sales pipeline and the size, as well as the number of sales contracts we'd signed.
- Cash availability versus total monthly expense, which would trend downward if we had poor sales performance.
- Customer implementation time, that is, how long it took our clients to adopt our solutions.
- Projected delays in receiving cash we were owed. Seeing this in black and white encouraged us to meet our delivery deadlines, so we wouldn't be causing the lag.
- Our Accounts Receivable (AR) compared to our expectations.
- Then we asked questions about each metric:
    - Based on each metric, will our cash forecast be going up or down?
    - What behaviors do we need to change to improve these metrics and therefore our cash forecast?
    - How does this affect our behavior and our cash situation?
    - How does it help us drive our cash upward?
    - What does it mean for our cash flow? Will our cash rise or fall as a result?

Next, we put together the Stop Signs Dashboard. Each of the three colors—Green, Yellow, and Red—had their own specific success criteria. Our actions would be guided by this dashboard. If the indicators were Green, we could continue our current spending and rate of growth. If the indicators turned Yellow, our growth was causing faster spending than our cash flow could support, and that wouldn't be sustainable. We would need to slow down and consider our expenses without hurting our people. Red meant that we needed to take immediate action before we ran out of cash.

This level of clarity allowed me to involve the right people in deciding the status of each indicator. Once we knew what we needed to know, we knew the right question and whom to ask.

But that wasn't the end of the process. Patrick pushed me to figure out what we'd do if a certain indicator turned Yellow or Red. Why decide this in advance? Well, cash is like oxygen. If we are running out of it, we would be stressed and might not be able to think straight. Most of us can't propose thoughtful, innovative solutions in the midst of a crisis. Running out of money is like being asphyxiated, and an oxygen-starved brain can't find the way forward.

So, we discussed specific action plans if the indicators turned Red or Yellow and agreed that we would execute on these action steps.

I wish this was the end of the story. We had the right indicators, the right people providing actionable data, and an agreed-upon plan for tricky eventualities. But building a dashboard is a lot easier than putting it into action. That's something I found out as soon as an indicator turned Yellow.

I did nothing. I knew I was looking at Yellow and exactly what that meant—the dashboard is a pretty simple system, after all—but I found myself thinking, "Nah, it'll all work itself out. Growth is strong and sales continue to look good." I decided that if anything got worse, we'd be more than capable of pulling our irons from the fire in time.

Then the indicator hit Red. I'd been watching the data come in, and though we were working hard to solve our cash flow issues, we were not able to avoid turning Red. I knew what we had to do, because we had already discussed, debated, and decided in advance.

We still felt the need to review and debate if the plan of action was really necessary. I guess we all wanted to avoid taking drastic measures. Finally, my business partner, David, asked, "Why are we wasting time discussing this now? We're all freaked out and uncertain. Let's just pull out the plan we agreed to with Patrick and put it into action. Otherwise, what was the point of writing it?"

Our head of sales also proposed a delay. There were a couple of upcoming deals that might close the gap. But they weren't a certainty, and we couldn't predict exactly when that cash would arrive. Eventually, everyone saw there was no alternative to enacting the original plan.

So that's what we did. We put the plan into action and laid off sixteen people. That was the only way we could have made payroll and continued running the business. During my next coaching session with Patrick, I shared how the dashboard had saved AvidXchange. "If we'd waited two more weeks," I remember telling him, "we would have run out of cash." The new deals did eventually close but not in time to provide the cash we needed.

Today, we're a public company, something of which I'm immensely proud, but that wouldn't be true if we hadn't survived that crisis. The key to our survival was our simple early warning system, the Stop Signs Dashboard.

Patrick is an intensely curious person, and he was keen to derive insights from our near-death experience. I remember him telling me, "There is no wisdom in the second kick of the mule." We debriefed and learned the following:

- Our leading indicators and early warning system worked. I was focused on growth and very optimistic about the future, so it was hard for me to see reasons why we would tap the brakes. That was my blind side. Yours will be different, but I am sure you have a blind side. We all do. Our dashboard worked for us, but it was not designed for you.
- Our criteria for each leading indicator weren't based on feelings but on information that we could observe. This provided objectivity that ensured alignment on the Green, Yellow, and Red criteria. David and I have different emotional reactions and intuitions, so agreeing on those criteria in advance was critical.

We would not have been able to achieve agreement in the middle of our cash crunch.

Looking Ahead to Avoid a Crisis

In the spring of 2020, Bob Potter was taking a long, hard look at his Early Warning Dashboard. The COVID-19 pandemic was just starting, and Bob's early warning system was already predicting slower sales and an upcoming cash crunch in his database monitoring software company, SentryOne.

"We were doing great," he recounted. "We were focused, accountable, and delivering strong growth results. That's something you helped us with," he reminded me. "Your system kept us on track, and the business was humming along nicely. We had 180 employees, mostly based in Charlotte. At the time, we were running on a cash flow break-even basis, making zero profits and just putting everything back into the business to create growth." It was working. SentryOne was rapidly acquiring new customers and growing at 35 percent a year. Bob had been hiring for growth, and now his leading indicators were predicting that SentryOne would have too many people because of sales being reduced by the COVID-19 pandemic.

"We didn't have a lot of cash in the bank, so we approached our main investor for help." But investors were cautious. "They told us we had to run on the cash we had." This meant that they could no longer run the business at a negative cash flow with investors funding their growth. They had to find a way to get profitable fast, even if it meant sacrificing growth.

"No one knew how long this would last, so we had to take a short-term, almost myopic view." With the survival of SentryOne on the line, they were forced to make the painful decision to reduce their staff. "We got together and collectively made the decision to reduce our workforce from 180 to just 108, with a combination of layoffs and furloughs." Bob tried everything else before having to accept that 40 percent of his workforce was about to exit the company, either temporarily or permanently.

The staff reduction allowed SentryOne to survive the COVID-19 pandemic and become profitable. Six months later, it was time to bring back the twenty-six employees who were on furlough. During a coaching session, I asked, "Bob, how many of the twenty-six employees does the business really need?"

"Well, the problem is that we do not have enough work for all twenty-six employees who are scheduled to return from furlough. Our leading indicators show that we only have enough work for six of them." He sighed.

Emotionally, Bob was committed to bring back all twenty-six employees who were on furlough. But his early warning system clearly showed that he did not have enough work to justify doing this. Bob was struggling because he did not want to go back on his commitment. Bob already knew that the company could not afford to bring

back all twenty-six furloughed employees. At times like these, having a coach to talk through the difficult decision, why it has to be made, and how to follow through after making it really helped Bob to make the right decision.

Bob's early warning system gave him a CEO control tower. The system saved him not once but twice. Making these tough but necessary decisions helped SentryOne emerge from the COVID-19 crisis a much healthier company. In 2021, SentryOne's profitability was critical in attracting SolarWinds to purchase the company, giving investors and employees a strong return on their investment.

Letting employees go is one of the hardest things a CEO has to do. Nobody wants to do it, and many of these changes happen too late. But Bob had his early warning system to push him to make the right tough decisions. He acted in time to save the company and put it on a path to recovery as the crisis abated. His early warning systems saved his company so that it could grow and succeed.

BOTTOM LINE

1. Invest the time to build an early warning system: the Stop Signs Dashboard.

2. Be aware of the tyranny of the urgent. Other things may look more pressing right now, but the dashboard will help you to think critically to avoid potential disaster.

3. Don't be fooled by good current results. You need to look ahead to make sure you can deliver great results again and again.

4. Protect your blind side. Avoid potential issues by using leading indicators that can predict and alert you to possible train wrecks. Keep them future focused and predictive.

5. Begin with clear success criteria. Avoid rework and wasted resources. Don't start any project until you can describe what success looks like using simple Red-Yellow-Green success criteria.

6. Be transparent and engage all available brains. Share candidly what the real problems are while allowing teammates to engage their abilities to solve the problems.

7. Tackle problems, not people. Keep your team out of the foxhole of self-preservation with a focus on the problem, not whose fault it is.

8. Reward results, not effort. Avoid the common mistake of rewarding long hours and superhuman effort. Reward team members for achieving agreed-upon success criteria, and celebrate accomplishing stretch goals.

CHAPTER 8

ACHIEVE FULL ALIGNMENT

"Coming together is a beginning. Keeping together
is progress. Working together is success."

–HENRY FORD

My wife, Pei-Yee, and I were driving from Charlotte, North Carolina to Seattle, Washington. We had two choices of route. One took us west on I-90 to visit Glacier National Park in Montana. The other meant exiting the I-29 early and taking the I-80 toward Salt Lake City, Utah. Both routes involved about forty hours of driving, so the only real question was, which sights did we prefer to see?

Pei-Yee wanted to see Utah, but I wanted to visit Montana. However, we didn't talk about it. We both knew we were headed for Seattle, so neither of us felt the need to discuss how we were going to get there. After all, it's a long drive. We figured we would discuss our options and make decisions along the way.

But, as it happened, when we reached the decision point on I-29, Pei-Yee was driving, and I was asleep in the passenger's seat. She took I-80 toward Salt Lake City without realizing that I was looking forward to visiting Glacier National Park. I woke up and soon realized where we were.

"Wait ... what happened? We're heading to Utah on the 80?"

"That's right," she told me from the driver's seat.

Still rubbing my eyes, I said, "I thought we were going to take I-90 to Montana?"

"Montana? I didn't know that was the preference. But Salt Lake City would be a nice stop, right? And, anyway, this is the shortest route."

"Well, not really. The drive through Montana is the exact same distance and time according to Apple Maps, and I thought it would be great to visit Glacier National Park."

"Hmm, we didn't talk about that, so I took I-80 toward Salt Lake City." By this time, the decision was nearly an hour old, so backtracking would cost two hours and extra fuel. And that's if we decided quickly; I could easily imagine another half an hour of debate before we agreed on what to do. Every minute we spent debating and discussing would mean a longer drive to backtrack and take the other route. In the business context, it would have meant rework and waste. So I reset my own expectations and looked forward to visiting Salt Lake City.

This is a good example of being aligned on the destination or the final result but not taking the time to discuss and get aligned on the journey, how we are going to get there. Misalignment on the "how" often leads to unmet expectations, rework, or waste. In the example I shared, neither way was better. We just had different preferences.

FULL ALIGNMENT

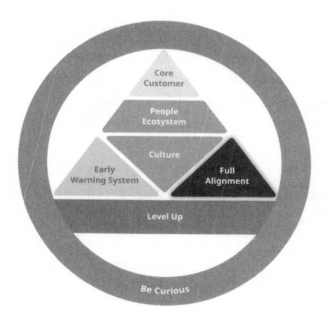

A common mistake is getting aligned only on the final outcome while believing that how the team executes toward that final outcome is not important. You may also believe that the different tasks and projects leading to execution can be easily delegated without much discussion.

Aligning only on the desired results or final outcomes often leads to misunderstandings along the way.

I've seen this happen often with senior leaders. They agree on the result or destination and therefore believe that they are aligned and can move on to something else, expecting their teams from different departments to work in alignment. A month or two later, they realize that different teams were not in synchronization in their work. They wonder how this happened, and frustration begins to build because they are encountering rework, waste, and a renegotiation of deadlines. Time sensitivity and the pressure to make the right decision regarding reallocating work and the possibility of impacting other projects add to the frustration. The pressure to decide might even cause more mis-alignment as teams begin to make decisions that benefit their own teams without thinking about the company as a whole.

They agreed on the "what" but did not discuss expectations for the journey. They did not agree on the "how."

FULL ALIGNMENT IS ABOUT HOW WE GET THINGS DONE, NOT JUST WHAT WE WANT TO GET DONE.

Full alignment is about *how* we get things done, not just what we want to get done. The crucial mistake we make is in stopping our discussions when we have achieved alignment on what we want to do and by when. We don't spend time discussing how we are going to get there.

This chapter is about helping you to identify when you are mis-aligned and how to attain full alignment. Full alignment will reduce mistakes and waste, and it will help you achieve your final outcomes while improving relationships.

MISTAKES THAT CAUSE MISALIGNMENT

Mistake #1: Mistaking Abdication for Delegation

Here is an example of abdication: "Here's the project, here's the result I want, and here's the time frame. The rest is up to you. Enjoy yourself and let me know when it's done." At first glance, this looks like good delegation. You have made clear what the project is, the results you want, and the time frame. What is missing are discussion and visual-ization of what needs to be done along the way. What are the necessary milestones so that we all know that the work is being done according to expectations? Without this discussion, you won't be able to inspect what you expect along the way. You won't be able to provide any coaching or assistance for troubleshooting if things don't go well. In fact, without clarity on how the project should be done, you won't even know if things are going well until the project's end date. You will then be met with a pleasant surprise or an unpleasant surprise.

And if the project is delayed, as many projects often are, the employee might feel unsupported by their leader because you were not able to provide direction or coaching along the way.

Delegation, on the other hand, means saying, "Here's the result we want. Let's discuss your approach and the critical milestones so that we will know if you are on track or need some assistance." Don't go too far by dictating exactly how to get the work done. Coach the employee by asking them to visualize how they will work on this project. Ask for milestones so that you can inspect the work, hold them accountable to succeed, and provide coaching or feedback as necessary.

The key lesson is to discuss and agree on how we are going to achieve success. It's the "how," not the "what," that allows full alignment to happen. Milestones help us discuss and visualize how the work is going to be done. This is the agreed-upon journey we can be held accountable to.

Leadership is a full-contact sport. Your job is to keep your team aligned with you continuously and to be there to provide guidance, feedback, and coaching for them to succeed. Your job is not to come in at the end and judge whether they succeeded or failed. If you are surprised that they succeeded or failed at the end of a project, then you abdicated instead of delegated.

IF YOU ARE SURPRISED THAT THEY SUCCEEDED OR FAILED AT THE END OF A PROJECT, THEN YOU ABDICATED INSTEAD OF DELEGATED.

Mistake #2: Not Agreeing on Process

Another common mistake happens when leaders agree on the outcome but have different methods or processes for pursuing that outcome. This is the same problem Pei-Yee and I experienced when we agreed to drive to Seattle but did not discuss and agree on the route we would take ahead of time. Full alignment happens when you have also discussed and agreed on the process to achieve the agreed-upon outcomes. When leaders have not agreed on the process, what ensues is confusion from their team members. This confusion causes team members to question if their leaders are aligned or, even worse, to assume that they are not. This breakdown causes stress and drama and makes collaboration difficult across teams.

MICHAEL'S PERSPECTIVE

I hired Steve, a senior executive with lots of experience. Steve had managed six thousand people at eBay and had a depth of experience that would be very helpful to AvidXchange. We started off great together. I was very excited about having a steady and experienced hand like Steve's by my side. And Steve was enthusiastic about making a difference in a smaller company. He knew he had the experience to help me and the team negotiate difficult situations as we scaled up that he had seen before. Steve was going to save us from some of the mistakes that he had already experienced.

Steve and I had the best intentions, but we had different approaches. Our different approaches and processes led to misalignment on how to get the job done.

Steve and I started hearing from employees that they felt we were not on the same page. Yet, we got along great! So I went to Steve and made sure that we were aligned regarding our goals and desired outcomes. We believed that our employees were mistaken and that we needed to educate them on how we were aligned on projects that had to be finished and the desired outcomes and timelines. We both went about reassuring everyone that we were indeed aligned and working together toward the same goals.

But this problem persisted for many quarters. Work was still getting done, but stress was also building, and we could not get past the chatter that Steve and I were not aligned. It was confusing to us and frustrating.

Sometime later, Patrick asked me to reflect on what had happened. "Now that time has passed, and with the benefit of hindsight, what do you think really happened? I know you respected Steve and vice versa, so how come we could not get this to work?"

Steve and I both really liked each other, but we had different methods. And I wanted to learn from him. I believed his experience was strong and that he could help us scale up AvidXchange to thousands of employees. We had to go where he had already walked. So I was convinced that we needed him, and we also needed to change and adapt as we grew. Some things that we thought were working now might not work in our future. Maybe there was a better way, and Steve would be able to lead us forward. But we had disagreements on a few fundamental points of the process of running the business that surfaced as we worked together. These were the cause of perceived misalignment by our team members.

Here is an example: We have a strong weekly rhythm to how we run AvidXchange. We meet every week and discuss how our priorities for the quarter are faring. We provide a Green, Yellow, or Red status. We discuss the yellows and reds and consider adjustments we need to make to get back on track or to stay on track to accomplishing our goals. We have followed this process—the process that Patrick taught us—since the beginning of time at AvidXchange. Steve believed that these weekly meetings and adjustments were too frequent. He felt that we needed accurate data on a monthly basis and that we should consider an adjustment or change only after collecting two months of data. Steve believed that if we acted on the wrong data and made adjustments weekly, we might discover later that we were incorrect and change back. This would cause whiplash. And our team members were already sharing that, oftentimes, their priorities changed before they could complete a project. Steve believed that our current practice would contribute even more to the changing priorities that people were feeling as we grew bigger. But I had experienced how a small, uncorrected mistake can cause a much larger deviation over time. I wanted us to continue being very proactive at staying on track with our goals and making the necessary adjustments if we started drifting off course.

We never did get aligned or reconcile this difference in process. We tried to compromise and respect each other's position.

I thought that what Steve said made a lot of sense. And I was wondering if I was clinging to something old that should be changed. But my instincts told me that our weekly rhythm would continue to make our company successful. It would allow us to scale up.

I wanted to try Steve's system, but I was not willing to give up mine. So, I still asked people to provide a weekly status for their work, while Steve told them not to spend their time that way for the sake of efficiency. There were no bad guys here—just both of us doing the best we could with what we knew. Looking back, I can understand why the team kept insisting that we were not aligned. We were asking for different things on a daily basis, so it felt misaligned even though Steve and I were totally aligned on what we were trying to accomplish at the end of the day.

We tried hard to make it work. Steve suggested a compromise of moving my weekly rhythm to every two weeks. I agreed but, again, was not completely sold on doing that. Compromising in this situation helped us to avoid what Patrick refers to as a Spicy Discussion. Instead of compromising, we should have had the Spicy Discussion and wrestled our disagreement around the process to the ground. We should have chosen one path and gotten aligned on our process.

The lesson here is that we were fooled by our alignment and agreement on final outcomes and desired results. But we did not achieve full alignment, because the process maps out how we should actually do the work. Process affects all our team members. Not aligning on how to do the work caused a lot of stress and drama.

Mistake #3: Failing to Communicate Your Vision Frequently

Sometimes misalignment happens simply because people forget. They forgot what you shared. Yes, it was exciting to hear the vision for the year at the company kickoff meeting. But they all went back to their daily work and forgot all about it.

Jack, like many other CEOs, shared his frustration with me that his people seemed to forget what they needed to achieve as a company for the year. He shared with me that he was tired of repeating himself. Unfortunately, people are too busy working for you to remember what you want them to remember.

I shared with Jack that as leaders, we need to be prepared to repeat our themes and mantras. In fact, most leaders have thought about what they want to share over and over again in their heads. You've probably turned the idea over a few hundred times in your mind, each time refining the message until you were completely satisfied with how it sounds.

Then we share it with our employees once, and we expect them to understand and feel as passionate about the message as we do. If you think about it, that's not really fair. You've heard the message in your own head a hundred times. How can you expect everyone else to get it perfectly the first time? You should expect to have to repeat the message, perhaps many times.

A few years ago, I was facilitating a planning session for Ratmir at Veeam. He shared the new marketing message that all his leaders must be able to share to their teams. Ratmir declared that before the day was out, we had to repeat this message naturally nine times during our planning session. It would be my job as the facilitator to make sure that happened.

"Ratmir, why nine times?" I asked.

"Because that is how many times it takes for the message to stick."

"I had heard before from my publicity coach that we had to repeat the message five or six times."

"No, that's wrong. You need to repeat the message at least nine or ten times. In fact, the more complicated the message, the more times you need to repeat it for everyone to get it. Our new message is very simple, so I need us to repeat it nine times today until it gets stuck in everyone's head."

Ratmir knew that it takes great intention and repetition to get any message across. Misunderstanding messages cause misalignment. After all, how can you get aligned if you do not even know the correct message?

FULL ALIGNMENT: HOW TO GET AND STAY ALIGNED

I have shared the mistakes that cause misalignment, and they happen without most of us knowing. The key takeaway lesson is that it is not good enough to get aligned on the goal or the desired outcomes. Full alignment happens when you are continuously aligned on the whole journey. You must align on the "how," not just the "what." I'd like to summarize the techniques for you to get and stay aligned.

Start with "Why"

Before starting a project, make sure everyone understands the importance of the work and the purpose behind the work.

Visualize the Journey Together

Go beyond getting aligned on a SMART (Specific, Measurable, Achievable, Relevant, Time-bound) goal. Take the time to discuss the approach, and visualize how you will get there together and what is expected from each participant for the project to be successful. This is just like my trip to Seattle with my wife or Michael's learnings about needing to get aligned on the process or on the "how" to get something done.

Commit to a Rhythm of Communication

Full alignment continues only if you realign regularly. Commit to a regular rhythm of check-ins that allow you to catch misalignments and correct them quickly. The question is not *if* you will become misaligned; rather, it is *when*. Having a regular rhythm of communication allows you to be proactive about getting realigned instead of waiting for something to go wrong that forces the conversation reactively. Reactive conversations come with more emotional attachment and drama. It's better to be proactive than reactive.

Use Weekly Meetings to Sync Up and Adjust

It does not take long to get misaligned. And if misaligned, it does not take long to make mistakes, resulting in waste, frustration, and rework. I recommend meeting weekly to check your team's alignment on important work. Weekly sync-ups provide the chance to gain insight and make adjustments early.

Run toward Conflicts Instead of Avoiding Them

Engage in Spicy Discussions. Difficult conversations are at the heart of misalignment. Just like spicy food, it burns when you dive in but only for a short time. It causes you to sweat and might even raise your heart rate. But it is so good once you get into it! You drink water, wipe away the sweat, and are grateful you tried that spicy dish.

Once you realize that there is a Spicy Discussion on the horizon, this means that misalignment has already happened. That's why the difficult conversation is necessary. But it feels unpleasant, and you begin making up a bunch of excuses to delay the conversation or avoid it altogether. Instead of thinking, "Uh-oh, that's a difficult conversation to have," you might want to change your point of reference and think, "Uh-oh, we are getting misaligned. And the longer I delay having a discussion to get realigned, the more people this affects, and the more painful and expensive it will be to fix in regards to time, resources, and damaged relationships. Time to get spicy!"

Unlike fine wine, these difficult conversations do not get better over time. They are more like rotting strawberries. They look good on the outside but are fermenting on the inside. And the longer you wait, the worse the rot inside becomes, and the more difficult and distasteful it is to eat.

UNLIKE FINE WINE, THESE DIFFICULT CONVERSATIONS DO NOT GET BETTER OVER TIME. THEY ARE MORE LIKE ROTTING STRAWBERRIES. THEY LOOK GOOD ON THE OUTSIDE BUT ARE FERMENTING ON THE INSIDE.

Engage in Active Realignment for
High-Change Situations

Some topics are really difficult to resolve completely because circumstances keep changing. The right decision for today might not be the right decision for tomorrow. If these changing situations affect many stakeholders, they can become exceptionally divisive. Such situations need to be discussed regularly to achieve alignment proactively. I refer to this as active realignment.

Back when Veeam was a lot smaller, they depended on VMWare as their main collaborator to sell their backup software. A key part of Veeam's portfolio was providing backup services for VMWare users. "It was 75 percent of our business," Ratmir remembered when we discussed it. "So, when VMWare said 'jump,' we had to ask 'how high'?"

Ratmir worried that VMWare might one day produce its own backup solution. He led discussions about how closely tied Veeam should remain to a fast-growing behemoth that could quickly render a key product obsolete. "There were tough discussions over the years," Ratmir remembered. "We were constantly asking ourselves, 'Do we try to own our own destiny, or do we continue to give in whenever VMWare wants something?'"

This was a difficult topic, the members of the executive team varied in their opinions. It would have been tempting to just insist that they had already made the decision on how to handle this situation in a previous discussion. But this would have been the wrong approach, because the situation was constantly changing because of Veeam's growth, VMWare's approach, and different executives at VMWare cycling in and out of the relationship with Veeam.

Ratmir shared, "Some people believed that VMWare was critical to our survival, so we should agree to their demands. Others believed that we were large enough to decide our own future, that VMWare should not be able to hold us hostage."

Veeam grew more and more successful every quarter. As Veeam got bigger, they developed more options. They needed their executive team to review and discuss new options and be flexible and nimble to make a different decision. Then they had to get everyone aligned and agree to the new direction. As their planning session facilitator, I made sure this topic was revisited every quarter during their planning sessions. I had to encourage everyone to have the patience to discuss this topic again, to be curious about learning more about the situation, and to be open to making a different decision.

"Yes, in those days, things could change in six or twelve months," Ratmir shared. "Circumstances change and we might end up being wrong. That's why I needed us to revisit our decisions on this topic every quarter so that everyone could get aligned and execute well." Ratmir's perspective here was the key. He was prepared to change based on what was happening. Too often, ego becomes attached to decisions, and that limits change as people become invested and entrenched. Ratmir's willingness to reflect the changing reality was very powerful, especially because that hard-won alignment would naturally come into question again after a quarter or two as VMWare made unexpected changes themselves.

"We had to get aligned again every quarter. An executive might not agree with the decision," Ratmir continued, "but they had to support it. Lots of companies don't even want to have that kind of discussion, where one group loves an idea but another group hates it." Ratmir had the courage to lead his team in this discussion during their quarterly planning sessions. They got realigned on this difficult topic every quarter. "Realignment was necessary and gave us clear communication to our employees. This is important to avoid them making up their own approach. We had to tell them our decision and plan, and they applied our approach and decision consistently across the company. I am referring to our teams in the field, marketing— everyone. Doing this well meant that we did not waste resources, and people were not making up their own choices about something that should be decided on a strategic level for the company."

Plan with Other Departments and Teams to Align Horizontally

As a company grows, silos build unintentionally as teams focus more on their own areas of responsibility. Processes take over and dictate how teams will pass projects in progress to other departments for completion.

As work becomes more specialized, it ironically also becomes more cross-functional. Initiatives to execute strategy are becoming enterprise-wide. So instead of being more focused on our own departments, we really need to come together and plan cross-functionally with other teams. The process of planning with other teams creates full alignment across departments. It reduces silos and aligns teams on how they are going to execute priorities across the company. Because work is becoming much more cross-functional, this type of planning and preparation to execute well as a company is now critical to minimizing mistakes and rework. We must recognize that our work impacts other departments. In many cases, handing work off to another team to deliver to a customer can cause delays if the other team did not expect that work to flow to them. Teams now need to have full alignment on when work will be done and by whom, especially for cross-functional projects.

It is concerningly easy to miss a customer delivery when the work is passed across multiple teams and departments. The only way to get it right is to visualize the work together in cross-functional planning sessions, where each team can sequence the work in their own teams in a way that comes together for the overall success of the project at the company level.

MICHAEL'S PERSPECTIVE

As we started scaling to a hundred million and beyond in revenues, we planned cross-functionally. Our planning process started with the executive team figuring out what our top five priorities are for the company every quarter. Each executive then took a stab at figuring out how these priorities cascade to their teams.

Next, each executive worked with their teams to get detailed plans developed. We then came back together, and each team shared their part of the plan, while other teams listened to see where collaboration was needed. This turned out to be important, because various team members did not always know when work was dependent on other teams. We did not realize how cross-functional some of these projects were. But our cross-functional planning approach helped to catch these dependencies and resolve them before they became problems or bottlenecks.

Planning cross-functionally with teams had the benefit of getting our teams truly aligned on how to execute the work every quarter. It helped us live our core value, "Win as a Team." Since we were hiring quickly, this practice also helped new employees learn the business faster as they learned about other departments' work during our planning process.

Making sure we get and stay truly aligned on how to get work done is still an important process for us as a public company today.

Frederique-Constant, a luxury Swiss watch company, was experiencing the conundrum of teams seemingly getting more efficient, yet their overall production of watches—their output—was actually slowing down. Upon close observation, it appeared that each department in the production line was focused only on their personal KPIs. Each step of the process seemed to have separated itself from the others. Every worker viewed themselves as successful in achieving their deliverable, as long as the person preceding them in the chain provided what they needed. They were not accounting for the delays that happened when the previous group was slow in delivering their pieces or when the previous team missed a deadline. Each team would start their clocks when they were handed their piece of the work.

They did not realize that the efficiency of the parts did not redound to the efficiency and effectiveness of the entire manufacturing process. So while their personal KPIs might have been Green, overall, as a whole team, they were not delivering enough watches.

When we discussed this at a planning session, they thought it was due to a lack of accountability. This is one of those rare occasions when accountability was the red herring. Each department was being accountable for their part of the delivery. However, they did not have full alignment.

To solve this problem, they had to slow down and take a departmental, collaborative approach. They had to visualize what it would take for the complete watch to be manufactured, not just what their individual teams had to do. When they started collaborating and getting aligned across departments, they began to see where they were not synchronized in getting the right parts on time to deliver fully manufactured watches. They found ways to help one another. Instead of believing their part was done and successful, they became invested in one another's success, and this sped up overall production.

The key lesson is that most projects these days are complicated and require the skill sets of people across the company. To get a project done, you naturally need to cross department lines. You can't work in a silo and achieve overall success for the company. When a team or department finds itself waiting on someone else, or if the next team is not ready to take your product and sell it, your company did not experience a win, even though you might have delivered your piece on time. When this happens, it is a symptom of horizontal misalignment.

We need to reach across the lines and get horizontally aligned for the overall success of the company. If the company does not win, you don't win either, even if you believe you achieved your desired outcomes in your department. We must learn to get horizontally aligned to win as a company.

.

BOTTOM LINE

1. Aligning only on the destination or desired results does not work. You must align on the journey as well as the destination. Align on the "how," not just the "what."
2. Align around clear goals that everyone understands and can repeat back to you.
3. Avoid abdication. Delegate by visualizing critical milestones. This allows you to inspect what you expect and stay aligned throughout the entire process.
4. The process is important. Not agreeing on the process can get you out of alignment and cause confusion.
5. Reiterate and repeat your goals. Be ready to do this more often than you'd imagined would be necessary.
6. Revisit decisions that are made in high-change scenarios. When things change, your teams will naturally get out of alignment.
7. Use weekly meetings to get realigned. Dive into the tough issues, get spicy when needed, and work to keep everyone's attention.
8. Enterprise priorities are becoming more cross-functional. Plan with other teams to make sure you achieve full alignment to remove misunderstandings and potential obstacles.
9. Reach across the lines to avoid silos. Communicate goals and progress regularly so that everyone is informed and ownership is shared.

CHAPTER 9

MAKE CULTURE YOUR COMPETITIVE ADVANTAGE

"For individuals, character is destiny. For organizations, culture is destiny."

–TONY HSIEH

Dave seemed like the perfect hire. He had a strong résumé filled with operational experience, and he had account management skills from his consulting experience with one of the large consulting firms. He had a warm personality and seemed to have good judgment. He also displayed the right core values during all our interviews. Convinced I had found the perfect candidate, I brought him on board as our chief operating officer.

After a few weeks, I noticed that Dave did not bring up any issues in our weekly meetings or our one-on-one meetings. I asked him specifically what issues he might be seeing in our operations, and his reply was always that things were going well and that I had nothing to worry about.

Finally, after about six weeks, I got very direct with Dave. "Dave, you need to be open with me and not hide issues from me. I am an operations-oriented CEO. We had problems that we had to solve before you got here, and I am convinced that we still have problems. Now, either you are stupid and can't see the problems, or you think I am stupid and don't know that you are hiding them. So which is it?"

Stunned by my directness, Dave answered slowly, "OK, we do have some issues, but nothing that is serious enough to rise to you, and nothing that I cannot handle."

"I did not ask you if there were crises or emergencies that you could not handle," I pushed further. "I am asking you what issues we might have and what problems we are working to solve."

I went on to share with Dave that our way of working at this company was to share issues openly and transparently. I believed that together, with more brains working on a problem, we would come up with the best solutions that the company had to offer and not be limited by any one single person's abilities or experience. I wanted him to begin sharing issues transparently at our weekly team meeting. Dave surprised me by sharing that he was not comfortable doing that. "Where I come from in the consulting world, I was trained to solve problems and bring the solutions to the consulting partners. It was unthinkable to share issues transparently without having solutions to these problems ready to be deployed. I don't think I can easily do what you are asking me to do. To share problems immediately with no solutions is just a very foreign concept for me."

"Well, Dave, I don't like surprises, and I don't like any one individual, including myself, to be a bottleneck in our company. I want openness, transparency, and collaboration to solve problems. I want to engage all the brains on our executive team. I realize this is really a shift in mindset that is needed. So I need you to think about this way of working and decide if you can make the shift. And if you cannot do that, I'd like your resignation by the end of the week."

Dave was shocked. "You're going to fire me over something small like this?" he asked.

"No, I am not going to fire you. I am offering you the dignity to resign at the end of the week. Because this is our way of working. And this is not a minor issue—it is huge. While I do appreciate the experience you bring from the big consulting firm, you don't work there anymore. You work here. Frankly, if you don't adopt this mindset, you won't enjoy working here, and you and the rest of the team will end up having a lot of friction. Let's not waste each other's time and energy struggling with that."

This was a very cordial discussion. There were no raised voices or anger. Dave came back at the end of the week and shared that he was amazed at this way of working and respected the way I discussed this with him. He already knew that he liked our culture and core values. He committed to try his best to change his way of working. While he did not know if he would succeed, he would give it his all. He asked me to observe him for four more weeks and help him make the shift. If he was not able to change his mindset after the four weeks, he would resign.

Dave stayed, made the shift, and turned out to be a strong member of our executive team.

YOUR CULTURE

That was over twenty years ago. What I did not realize back then was that this was a mindset problem. At the time, I thought it was a core values problem, but it was not. Dave actually lived our core values, but he had a different mindset on how to handle issues and problems. Back then, I called it our "way of working." Over time, I have realized that a "way of working" is made up of mindsets layered on top of core values. This combination of mindsets and core values determines how we behave and how we end up working together.

Your employees' behavior and how they relate and work with one another is the practical working culture of your company. Core values are part of it, but limiting the discussion to only core values does not give you the full picture of your company's culture.

Core values are the unchanging, fundamental principles that define the heart of your organization. These are the values that you would hold even if no one was watching you. You hope that all your employees will embody these values and demonstrate them in their actions on a daily basis.

Mindsets are the ways you think about and approach a situation or problem.

Think about how the values (core values) that you hold combined with how you approach situations (mindsets) determine how you react to situations at work (behavior). The practical side of culture comes down to how a company's employees behave and work with one another. Core values and mindsets collectively shape behavior.

BEHAVIOR = CORE VALUES + MINDSETS

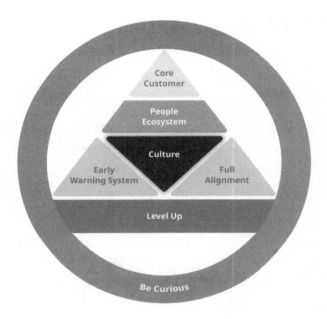

Your culture is the center of your company. If you get it right, your culture will attract and retain the right employees, and your journey will be much more enjoyable for everyone who signs up to join you. If you get it wrong, you will end up losing talent and wasting lots of energy. You will be constantly reinvesting in new hires.

BEHAVIOR DEFINES YOUR CULTURE

MICHAEL'S PERSPECTIVE

AvidXchange was experiencing hyper growth in 2015. It was an exciting time, with our core team of over four hundred employees growing to over a thousand in just a couple of years. Growth and change always bring stress, though, and I felt that the influx of new hires would test and perhaps transform AvidXchange's unique culture. We had a very strong mission and supporting core values, and we were relentless in hiring people who not only believed in our mission of "Transforming How Middle Market Companies Pay Their Bills" but also shared our core values. That was a key hiring principle.

My challenge was to hire a team of more experienced, senior people who also had the ability to build and support a business of over $100 million. We wanted to bring on board people who had already walked the path that we were about to take. I thought that seasoned executives would bring much-needed calm and stability during a time of incredible growth. I expected them to also bring scalable processes to make our growth easier for the existing team. Instead of us wandering around in a dark room, trying to find the light switches, I wanted to bring in people who already knew where the switches were. I wanted them to come in, flip the switch, illuminate the way forward, and get us there faster—and with less stress.

Michael was entering a critical stage of his journey. Hiring fast can be perilous, especially if his hiring team makes the mistake of prioritizing work skills over the company's culture. Remember: culture is the way we work, our behavior, and how we relate to one another. When a company adds people very quickly, extra time and effort are put into the hiring process. This effort must continue during the onboarding process to teach and transfer the working culture to new hires. If this is done poorly, culture breaks down, resulting in misunderstanding, rework, and waste. Most leaders understand this in theory but do not prioritize the necessary time and energy for this. This is hard work, and it does not happen naturally or automatically. If not done well up front, it will cost even more in time and resources to fix later. It's a "pay me now or pay me later" problem.

As AvidXchange embarked on its most vigorous growth period, Michael brought in strong talent, people who contributed to making the firm a success. But he also made some painful mistakes that he would like to help other CEOs avoid.

Because Michael was already paying attention to core values during interviews, they were very successful in hiring people who shared and committed to their core values.

New Mindsets Surprised Michael

MICHAEL'S PERSPECTIVE

This is how I learned that culture was not only about core values. I observed that many of our new hires had a different way of thinking and working. I think of these as mindsets. Many of them did not have mindsets that meshed well with what AvidXchange needed. This created a lot of stress.

We were not interviewing specifically for mindsets at the time. In fact, this is how Patrick and I learned about the power and importance of mindsets. One group seemed to think, "OK, AvidXchange is hiring me because they are a startup. They have not learned how to scale yet. I am coming in to fix them and help the company scale!" We already had four hundred employees and were already more than ten years old, so we were not a startup. But they came from very large companies with thousands of employees. So in their minds, AvidXchange was very small. Many of them had never worked for a startup, so their definition of "startup" was quite different from the existing employees' definition, especially those who had been here more than five years. Some of these long-tenured employees felt disrespected when new employees referred to AvidXchange as a startup because in their minds, they already built AvidXchange through the startup phase.

Then, there was a second group that had focused on scaling. Their mindset was that everything had to be built for scale; otherwise, we would waste time and energy reworking it later to make it scalable. But they were not flexible, and their mindset of scaling really slowed down our innovation and speed for delivering new features to customers. They worked hard to only release things to customers that were "fully baked" and battle-tested for scale. This trapped us in huge debates within the company regarding whether we should scale up what we already had or develop new products and approaches that were immediately scalable. Which approach might prove to be better?

Patrick reflected, "You guys did try. It was hard. And the teams did not have enough spicy debates on this topic of scalability. I recall the issues coming up, but different people would shut it down instead of leaning into the discussion. And I am not criticizing. It takes a lot of courage and energy to lean into these discussions, especially when deadlines are looming."

When we do not have these difficult discussions, the loudest voice or the status quo wins.

Then there was a third mindset that surfaced that added to the difficulties. People who'd come to us from much bigger companies looked at us the way an adult looks at a teenager: "You're not fully formed yet, and you need someone with big-company experience to set you straight." They took one look at our corporate culture and decided it needed to significantly evolve or even be replaced. They did not value the existing AvidXchange culture.

Many of these leaders then hired people they knew before, bringing in more of the mindset that they had. Soon enough, we had factions starting to form. Eventually, I could identify two camps: Old Avid and New Avid. That was the last thing I wanted. It was a painful time!

Fortunately, there was one group that came in with a mindset of curiosity and valuing what really worked. They were curious about what had made AvidXchange so successful and recognized that the company already had a strong and positive culture. They embraced the entrepreneurial mindset and valued the domain knowledge that our early-stage members had accrued. In addition to having a mindset of curiosity, they were also nondualistic thinkers. They were able to hold competing ideas in their minds, pause, and create a third or fourth solution that was made up of the best of both competing ideas. It's what Patrick refers to as "the power of the A-N-D": taking pieces of option A as well as pieces of option B to create option C or D.

These were expensive lessons. Many of the leaders with the mindsets that did not mesh well have already moved on. They didn't like working for us and didn't appreciate the chaos that a high-growth company creates. I felt sorry for them, because I think the opportunity to be part of what we're doing is just fantastic. Others moved on because it just wasn't working; they had a hard time operating in a resource-constrained company that had limited budgets to make the level of investment that many were accustomed to making.

We lost people in this battle of mindsets. Some departures were necessary, but not all. We also lost a lot of tribal knowledge about our company and our way of doing business. Those people are incredibly hard to replace, and when they leave, it's a real setback. We still achieved our strategic goals and growth targets, but there would have been a lot less pain and expense if we'd hired people with the right mindsets.

In such instances, leaders think about the pain and waste. But the cost is even greater than they imagined as they often do not recognize the opportunity cost of making these mistakes—how the negative energy and wasted resources could have been used to achieve so much more. Opportunity cost is something that is very hard to quantify.

From this experience, I learned that culture is really about the intersection of mindsets and core values, resulting in the various behaviors that work to further define and evolve your culture. Hiring people with the right mindsets and core values will result in the right behavior and culture. What I did not realize in the beginning was how important mindsets are to the working culture of a company. People with the right mindsets helped us move forward faster. They were the wind in our sails. But people with the wrong mindsets set us back. They were anchors, slowing us down.

Why Culture Is Even More Important Now

For years now, consultants have been telling us that culture is really a strategic weapon. As long ago as 2006, Peter Drucker gave us the famous quote, "Culture eats strategy for breakfast." He didn't mean that we should ignore strategy and focus purely on culture. But he believed that many companies were ignoring the power of culture and the strategic advantage it can provide. By "culture," he meant much more than the beanbag chairs, free drinks, and pinball machines in the office. He meant the patterns of human behavior that exist among your employees and how these patterns can contribute to success.

Virtually every CEO now understands that culture is important, but many don't yet understand it from a competitive standpoint. Times have changed. Culture is finally truly a competitive advantage. Leaders who do not understand this will make terribly expensive mistakes.

Michael has always embraced culture as a competitive advantage. This is why he was able to learn, survive, and then thrive from his experience. In a strong economy when everyone has tailwinds driving their growth engine, culture can be overlooked. However, when an economic downturn sets in, culture becomes magnified as a true competitive advantage in attracting the best talent and—most importantly—in retaining the talent you need to achieve your next key milestones.

A company's culture defines how people work together and relate to one another. It's a mix of expectations, rules, traditions, and norms. These elements can be brought together intentionally, or a culture can emerge by itself. Michael and I observed that the culture of a workplace is defined by mindsets and core values that produce certain behaviors. Culture determines how your employees will feel about coming to work. In the current post-COVID environment, more employees are interested in working remotely, creating a culture that transcends the physical office. This has added a new dimension to how every company must think about their culture.

People can love or hate a company's culture, or they can be neutral about it. If they love it, they'll become engaged and inspired. To me, that sounds like the ideal employee.

If they hate it, they will either endure it or leave. Enduring it is even worse than leaving. Who wants to work with a dispassionate team member who is just enduring their time at work? Those are the people who bring down morale and who will eventually become obstacles to other people's efforts.

If they're neutral about it, you might see passive-aggressive behavior, where an employee expresses their disdain or discomfort indirectly. The return on payroll for people in this mood is pretty poor. They're likely only to do what they're asked to and no more. Furthermore, teammates who are neutral about a company culture will not be additive in terms of advancing the culture, and over time, their neutrality actually erodes the positive elements of the culture.

The culture of a workplace determines if your employees will enjoy being there, and in turn, that defines whether the company will get the best from them. "The economy will go up and down," Michael shared when we discussed the state of things in 2022, "but when jobs are available, people won't be afraid to move on because they don't enjoy the culture they're working in. This means that your team needs to really like coming to work, and that's all about building a culture they enjoy."

EMERGING TRENDS

For over twenty years, Michael and I have collaborated to make AvidXchange a great place to work. We've noticed some huge changes in that time, especially in how employees choose where to spend their careers. We have observed some emerging trends.

- *Passion and interests:* The younger generation of workers are courageous enough to follow their passions and interests instead of being funneled into jobs they're "expected" to do. Focusing on the joy of the work itself, rather than maximizing their compensation package, means they're less willing to work in unpleasant environments or do work that they do not enjoy. They are even less willing to tolerate toxic colleagues.
- *Flexibility to work from home:* The COVID-19 pandemic caused many people to rethink why they go to work and to gain a new appreciation for working from home, flexibility, and the preciousness of life itself.
- *Prioritizing life over work:* A new prioritization seems to be taking hold. People are seeing work as just one element of

their lives, and they are thinking very intentionally about the work they want to do. It's less common for employees to consider sacrificing their personal preferences—family, hobbies, travel—to secure the job they want. Rather than the outdated idea of "work-life balance," employees are beginning to design their lives in a very intentional way.

- *Empowered decision-making:* Employees are becoming more empowered, better informed, and motivated to make good moral choices, which also enhance their communities. They want to be part of something bigger than themselves. They do not want to choose between a good job and an impactful life. They are beginning to realize that they can have both.

- *Making a difference:* Employees have become increasingly interested in finding the company that fits them best. They want to connect to the mission and purpose of the company and contribute to the firm's success using their skill set. It's not just about a paycheck but about making a difference in the world along with having the ability to grow their careers.

- *Compensation beyond salary:* While still important, salary is only one part of the compensation system. We need to view compensation more holistically. Time off, flexibility, and contributing to social causes can also be viewed as compensation. Michael has found that employees are searching for more sustainable kinds of satisfaction. That's where corporate culture comes in. Don't misunderstand me—you still must pay people fairly. Pay is still an important part of the compensation equation, but it is not the *only* part.

Studies are showing that a firm's culture is a major factor when employees decide whether to stay or move on. "When someone leaves," Michael shared, "it's not necessarily a judgment but a statement of preference. It's not about the company, necessarily—it's about them. The working environment you've created might be ideal for someone else. But employees are making that call with greater confidence and intentionality than ever before."

GREAT TALENT HAVE GREAT OPTIONS

MICHAEL'S PERSPECTIVE

People are voting more with their hearts than their wallets. They want to work for companies where they feel purposeful and like they're contributing in a way that's meaningful to them.

Culture is finally becoming a real competitive advantage. There are now more high-quality jobs chasing people than in the past. With the explosion of innovative companies, there is so much competition for talent—especially technology-related talent. Today in the United States, we have a significant shortfall of qualified talent across almost all of the most relevant technology skill sets. This means that talented people have a lot more options now than before. Startups are going to find it hard to compete for talent when it comes to salaries. They are going to have to figure out how to use culture to win the right talent.

It's also becoming more common that people continue to search after accepting a job offer and then renege on the original offer because they found an even better fit. Previously, that was not an acceptable practice. But today, colleges are counseling their students to create more options for themselves by using this method. This is because there are more great jobs chasing great people, not the other way around. If you're talented and have the right skills, there are huge opportunities for you.

We saw this at AvidXchange, too. Some people just didn't show up for their first day. It was frustrating and rude. But it taught me something, too. We had to continue raising our game, getting our mission, purpose, core values, and mindsets out there as part of our recruitment, so that we'd attract the people who'd follow their hearts and minds to AvidXchange.

Part of the new power and intentionality we're seeing among potential employees comes from their recent experiences. Young people are more passion oriented. They watched the generations before them working too hard, and they don't want to do that. They're looking for something they can believe in and also to get home to their families at 5:30 p.m. Twenty years ago, people complained about their work-life balance all the time, but there was nothing they could do about it. Now, firms have to make room for people to leave the office in time to catch their kids' soccer game. That's not a bad thing. It's not capitulation. What's good for an employee's life is also good for the company.

At AvidXchange, our culture was always good, but now it's actually a competitive advantage. If our people are passionate about the company and love working in our environment, they get inspired and engaged. Our culture has made us "sticky," as we call it–the right people for us won't want to leave.

We're also seeing social media platforms like Glassdoor give a peek into a company's culture and how it feels to work there, as well as the recruitment process. Candidates are coming to us better prepared. It's all part of a major shift. For the first time, we're seeing them ask about the corporate culture, about staff cohesion, about volunteering opportunities, long before any discussion about salary or even benefits. They're able to research the company in more depth than ever before.

On top of that, existing employees have new ways to reveal the company's inner workings, in public or in private, and even to become whistleblowers if something is truly wrong. It's transforming the world of recruiting. That's why I really believe that a company's culture has to be a competitive advantage. Otherwise, they are losing out on hiring the best talent in their industry.

To get your culture right, you first must get your core purpose and your core values right. The purpose of a company comes from the founders. As the founder of AvidXchange, I need to explore questions about why I started the company and how I create meaning in my work. I owe a lot to Jim Collins (and his book *Good to Great*) in this sense. What I learned from Jim Collins, and from others, is that I had to decide what I was passionate about, as founder and CEO of the company. How do I contribute to the world and to society? Why is it meaningful to work at AvidXchange? You have to start with the "why." That helps you form a clear and inspirational answer. That's a great way to define your core purpose.

And then there are core values. Patrick taught me, many years ago, to make my values simple phrases that are easy to remember and to use regularly. That's worked well for us. Our core values are "Be passionate about customer success," "Win as a team," "Innovate to change the game," "Invest and spend wisely," "Play to our strengths," and "Have a blast." They're simple enough that you can bring them up in any kind of conversation, and they're not just corporate jargon.

Your core values should also give you an easy way to affirm the right behavior. For example, to emphasize how important it is to do something special for a customer, we might say, "Hey, let's add this feature because the customer needs it. We've got to be passionate about customer success." If we can work our core values into our daily language, that helps connect values to our actual behaviors.

PEOPLE ARE NOW VOTING MORE WITH THEIR HEARTS THAN THEIR WALLETS. IF WE CAN WORK OUR CORE VALUES INTO OUR DAILY LANGUAGE, THAT HELPS CONNECT VALUES TO OUR ACTUAL BEHAVIORS.

A CORPORATE CULTURE SUCCESS STORY

Ratmir Timashev, co-founder of Veeam, really got this right. He is a part of a very rare group of entrepreneurs who have grown a billion-dollar company without depending on outside financial investors. We can learn a lot from Ratmir.

Ratmir shared, "Instead of choosing corporate buzzwords that are not specifically meaningful to us, you suggested that we choose words we would use regularly when talking with employees." Ratmir said, "We searched for genuine words and phrases that we could use in our day-to-day conversations. We landed on: 'One Team,' 'Innovate and Iterate,' 'Veeam Speed,' 'Everybody Sells,' and 'Conversation from the Heart.'" This last one means that Veeam's employees are encouraged to be direct but nice.

Veeam's culture comes from Ratmir and his partner, Andrei Baronov. "My business partner, Andrei Baronov," with whom Ratmir co-founded Veeam in 2006, "has slightly different values from mine, but there's lots of overlap. He comes from the product side, so he's a bit more conservative. For him it's, 'under-promise but over-deliver.' Many companies are the opposite when it comes to capabilities. They want to check the marketing box and quickly release the functionality because it looks like what their customers want. But Andrei really understands how to create products which are successful for our customers." It seemed that the journey of aligning their core values was ongoing, depending as much on their background and temperament as their business experience. Undeniably, though, the behaviors on display at Veeam flow from the founders' own conception of how to work, build, reach customers, and succeed.

"We worked on the language of the core values for two or three quarters and refined them in our quarterly planning sessions. By the end of the year, we were confident that we had discovered our core values and worded them correctly, so we rolled it out to the whole company at our 2017 Annual Kickoff sessions in the US, Europe and Asia." Just like Michael, Ratmir has found that his core values are a lot more than just inspiring words to put on the wall. "Our values proved so important in driving results over the next few years. We had simple words and really simple ways to explain each value." This made the vital task of educating his people easier. This process isn't automatic. "We must have intentional discussions about the behaviors our core values are supposed to encourage. Working this way helped us grow quickly to over $1 billion in revenues by 2020."

YOU DON'T CREATE YOUR CORE VALUES. THEY WERE ALREADY THERE. I HAD TO DISCOVER THEM, AND THEN CLARIFY THEM AND CHOOSE THE BEST WORDS TO COMMUNICATE THEM.

Ratmir provided additional insights: "What I learned is that you don't create your core values. They were already there. I had to discover them, then clarify them and choose the best words to communicate them. To discover them, we asked people 'What does Veeam stand for?' We talked to our employees about our relationships with customers, about how we do business, about our products and support. We tried to understand what Veeam's employees truly care about."

Deciding on your core values won't mean that everyone applies them all the time. It doesn't mean there's nothing left to decide, and new aspects will always emerge. "We're well known for rewarding hard work," Ratmir told me. "It's a fun culture. But looking back, we could have improved accountability. I was quite forgiving if a salesperson didn't fully deliver. I wanted to give people a second chance to succeed, another quarter to prove themselves. We have a great culture that helps us hire and retain people, and it could be better with a little more accountability."

Ratmir was curious enough to ask an outside firm to evaluate Veeam's culture. "We commissioned a study, and after spending a month with us, the report agreed that we needed more accountability, but that our culture was good, overall. People are excited to come to work, and they work well as a team. They believe in the product and they focus on the customer. There's a go-getter attitude. I'm proud of all those things, and our core values help keep our eyes in the right place as we grow and change."

CULTURE SHOULD ATTRACT OR REPEL

As people prioritize what they want in life and work, your work environment plays an even bigger role in attracting and retaining the right people. Your work environment or culture should not be attractive to everyone. Instead, be very clear what your work environment is like. Be able to describe it, and articulate it clearly so that people who want what you have to offer will be attracted to join you. And people who do not want what you have to offer can understand well enough and choose not to apply.

At the time of writing, two of the toughest places to land an engineering job are Elon Musk companies: Tesla and SpaceX. He's built a corporate culture of unremitting hard work, of driving his people to extraordinary efforts in search of ways to change the world. I know a lot of people who would not want to work there. However, there are still many people who want to work in that challenging environment. Those who want that kind of intense environment will apply. Those who aren't suited for it should not apply. Elon Musk decides what type of environment and culture he wants for his companies. People then decide if they want to sign up for that or not.

The lesson we can learn from Elon Musk is to be extremely clear about your work culture and you will be able to attract the right people. And if someone does not like your work culture, it is OK. They do not have to apply to work at your company. Don't judge them, and don't feel like you have been judged. The right people who will love your work culture will find their way to you. They will end up staying with you much longer and enjoy your journey with you.

MICHAEL'S PERSPECTIVE

Culture is neither good nor bad. There are no villains here. Instead, it's a good fit or a bad one. And if it's a bad one, that doesn't mean the person is bad. It just means they probably won't thrive in your company's environment. Even if they're very talented or skilled, they'll get frustrated over time and leave, which sucks because you've invested heavily in them. So, don't do that. Don't chase talent that doesn't fit well into your company environment and culture.

Culture is now an engine for attracting, retaining, and helping to develop your workforce. The departure of experienced people is an expensive regret. A consistent and well-understood corporate culture can help to avoid that loss of tribal knowledge.

START WITH CORE VALUES

When we talk about corporate culture, I think we mostly mean the set of common behaviors seen in a business or workplace. And how are those behaviors created? Through a mixing together of mindsets and core values. Most leaders don't yet realize that mindset is an important ingredient that drives behavior. In fact, it's just as vital as the core values of an individual or a company.

In my twenties, I walked into a client's conference room and saw that they had these beautiful posters on the wall with their core values. I said to the client, "Elaine, those values are awesome! They make me want to work here for years and years." And she laughed and said, "Oh, those? They're just posters. Nobody really knows what they mean. I don't think anyone here could tell you what our values are, even though they're hanging on the walls."

I was surprised and disappointed. For many years after that, I rejected the idea of formalizing my company's core values, let alone making posters about them. I thought doing so was a negative, not a positive. Yes, I threw the baby out with the bathwater—I was young and impressionable and did not have a coach to guide me. It was my first time leading a company.

After exiting Metasys, when I reflected on my wins and misses, I realized that I had been wrong about core values. We spend 70 percent of our waking hours at work, whether it's remote or in person. Core values and the behaviors they create come across in every interaction with our team members. We either enjoy that 70 percent of our waking time or dread it.

If someone dreads their working time, they're going to move on! Today, people are more in tune with how a firm's culture affects their life and experiences. They'll vote with their feet and go to companies that they enjoy. The more talented the employee, the more confidently they understand what they want out of life. This gives them belief that they can find a good situation somewhere else. They're much less afraid to move on if they're not enjoying a company's culture.

The behavior of employees is key, and behavior really comes from a combination of mindsets and core values.

LAYER IN MINDSETS

MICHAEL'S PERSPECTIVE

In the beginning, we focused just on our core values. In the last few years, I've realized that the way someone thinks is just as important as core values. These are their mindsets, their ways of thinking. And applying mindsets to core values really drives behavior.

This evolution in thinking came from the speed of our growth. We were constantly in a state of change management. That's about helping people to see the mindsets they have and then to change or adopt them as the company itself grows and changes. We needed to understand the gap between the mindset someone has now and the mindset we need for them to be truly successful in the company.

This realization about the importance of mindsets came along at the same time as my dilemmas about hiring more experienced senior people. Those were expensive mistakes that we did not want to repeat. So, we evolved our thinking and realized we needed to figure out what mindsets people have *before* recruiting them.

When it came to our current employees, we started to help them understand that the mindsets that had brought us huge success in the past weren't going to take us into the future.

Mindsets Can Change as the Company Grows and Changes

MICHAEL'S PERSPECTIVE

Mindsets are as powerful as core values, but sometimes core values are embedded within mindsets. And mindsets change over time. For example, as you're growing, there's a mindset just around survival as a business, and that's how you make decisions. But those may not be the right decisions for the long term. Getting a product to your customers as quickly as possible is a survival-based decision, but it's not scalable. We wanted to transition from the survival mindset to a "growth and scale" mindset.

Today, we need to look at the incorporation of operational excellence and think more about optimizing efficiency. These aren't things you can do at the beginning, when getting customers and revenue is the focus. Once we'd won those customers, we could get more into efficiency. That mindset had to shift from survival and revenue in the first place to efficiency and excellence later. Without that shift, we wouldn't have been as successful, and we'd have lost people. There were some employees who were frustrated because they didn't make this shift in mindset. But at that point in time, we didn't know how to educate them that this is a new mindset that's necessary at this new stage of our company.

The excellence and optimization side of the business can grow from maybe 10 percent of the equation to 40 percent. All the rest is still revenue focus and customer acquisition. And this relates to the growth mindset. It's not just about revenue growth. It's also about how you scale a business and create a balanced approach between operational excellence and revenue growth. We worked hard to find that balance.

People usually can't figure this mindset shift out on their own, so we must conduct change management. Employees will get frustrated and say, "Hey, the company isn't the same anymore!" and they'll think of leaving. Instead, if we can help them understand that it's not a core values problem but a mindset shift that's needed, they'll better understand the journey, and many will choose to stay.

When an employee can't adopt the right mindset, they typically become frustrated. They'll see everything around them changing and growing, quickly realize that they're in the wrong place, and opt out. For example, if we bring someone in from a larger organization, like a big bank, they might be toward the end of their career and have the mindset of "I'm highly skilled at providing this one function, and that's all I do." At this pace of change, their skill set will quickly become obsolete and they'll be left behind. Most people feel that happening. They see the writing on the wall.

This issue of shifting mindsets—or failing to shift them—was at the center of the "Old Avid/New Avid" problem. It was incredibly stressful. I heard people say that all I cared about was revenue growth. And I hated that. It was not as simple as people would like to think. We had to sacrifice some internal projects. Ultimately, we had to achieve a balance between the growth mindset and the operational mindset, especially as a public company. During our early rounds of investment, we had new people coming in who didn't value our culture and instead had an overbearing attitude: "You've hired me because you're just a startup and don't know how to scale, so now I'm here to fix you."

As the company grew, from a few hundred to a thousand people, we were working really hard on core values. We did not know about mindsets back then. It was the missing puzzle piece.

I should have hired people who were prepared to embrace what we'd already achieved—the entrepreneurship and the talent that had built Avid—because that's where you find the domain knowledge. This domain knowledge turned out to be our secret sauce in growing the company.

A leader with a really strong cultural understanding would have said, "OK, we've got people here who've brought Avid from nothing to something and others who have experience of working to scale things up. Let's finely balance the two." That would have worked better than an either/or approach. Then, the leadership needs to have self-awareness in a very complex space where there's a mix of the founders, some original people, and a bunch of new employees. Our most successful new senior hire was really intuitive and basically said to himself, "I'm experienced in building a sales organization, but most of those experiences aren't going to be relevant at AvidXchange. I need to understand this culture and these people and then slowly pick a handful of things I know will work to help Avid evolve and perform better."

Magic is created when you are able to leverage the rich experiences that define the history of a company along with the influx of new leaders who have the skill sets and experiences required to reach the next milestones of growth.

The right mindsets combined with core values create very powerful behavior. Here is an example. "Win as a Team" is one of our core values. "Curiosity and learning" is a mindset that helps to create the right behavior to be curious about one another's strengths and help us win as a team.

Each CEO needs to figure out what mindsets should be encouraged and combined with the company's core values to create the right behavior and working culture environment. These five are important to me at AvidXchange:

- **Growth Mindset.** This way of thinking means you're ready to be part of a growing business and all the change and chaos that means. Some people are energized by that, and others are freaked out and become paralyzed. You need a mindset that accepts and embraces growth and change. The failure risk there is that you can end up recruiting more for the mindset than the skill set.
- **Curiosity and Learning.** People with this mindset want to grow themselves and their careers. They enjoy being at a growing company and are passionate about growing themselves, too. If they aren't obsessive about it and are happy to stay in the same position for years, they're not going to do well at a growing company. This mindset has allowed us to continue growing, learning, and taking on every challenge that has come our way at AvidXchange.
- **Be Obsessive about Customers.** This applies to all parts of the company, not just the customer-facing teams. Legal, accounts department–every level, every part of the business, every employee.
- **Focus on Connecting with Teammates.** In a high-growth environment, you need to connect with real intentionality. That was especially true during COVID when people weren't in the office every day. Without that mindset, we'd have been at a major disadvantage. We really value being together, physically, in the same space. It feeds into our core value, "Win as a Team." And it's our best defense against siloed thinking.
- **Be Cross-Functional, Not Siloed.** Silos happen by mistake. They are created when one leader believes their projects are more

important than other projects. This causes an internal battle for resources, and leaders easily forget that the most important thing is the success of the company, not their individual or departmental projects.

CULTURE IS EVERYTHING TO JAY

In the last few years, Dr. Jay Cohen successfully merged Signature Consulting with Digital Intelligence Systems (DISYS) to create a $1 billion business as Dexian.

"I started the company," he shared with me from his home in Florida, "when I was still a practicing doctor. Everyone was saying that I should invest in the stock market, that I'd never be able to retire if I didn't invest. My brother did well as an investor. But my father had lost everything because of unscrupulous money managers. So, I looked around for a way to invest, and I got into investing in the staffing business."

Dividing his time between these two very different careers, Jay scheduled time at his new staffing office on Wednesday mornings and Friday afternoons. "I had four young people working for me. I was at the hospital, dealing with a ninety-year-old patient who had gallstones. Suddenly, I get this phone call from one of my guys at the office. They'd had to pull a guy off a job, and then the client canceled, and the guy was threatening to quit. I'm there trying to help this very old, very sick lady, and I told him, 'Look, I know we need to keep this guy, but I don't know anything about the business. Can't you handle it?' And he's close to panicking. He's saying, 'Jay, we're losing money every day on things like this. We gotta do something.'"

Jay tried a novel approach. "So I stepped outside of the problem, and said to myself, 'If I ran a body shop, or something like that, I'd just tell the guy there was nothing we could do. But what if we do something the body shop would never do? If I were that guy, what would I want to happen?' So I told my office, 'Call up so-and-so, and find this guy a new job. I don't care if we lose money on the contract.' He nearly choked, but he did what I asked, and I went back to fixing the old lady's gallstones. Then, the next day, when I came into the office, my guy asked me, 'Are you really serious about working that way?' And I said, 'Yes, or I'm out.'"

"And just like that, it became our mantra: 'Do unto others.' I said to them, 'This is what I believe, and this will help us build a successful business. And moreover, if we can't do these things, I don't want to be part of it.' People looked at you funny if you said you were always going to be honest. It was like, 'Wait, what's wrong with you? Everyone lies!' If the only way to be successful was to pretend to be honest, then I wasn't interested."

This realization has stood the test of time. "It's battling upstream," he admits. "And I'd never studied this stuff. I'd only ever studied medicine. But I've interfaced over twenty-five years with a tremendous number of people, and not one of them has ever knocked me off my belief that culture, in a certain sense, is next-to-everything, particularly when it comes to retaining employees and keeping customers. When I started the company, I didn't have any kind of directional guide. The only thing I knew was culture and my belief in a certain way of doing things in life."

Signature Consulting was built on those broad principles. "As we grew and we started to understand the business, it became more and more difficult but also, more important, not to veer from that path. It'd have been easy to cut a corner here, be expedient there, take the easy course rather than the hard course. We ended up in our meetings talking about how to live life, how to make choices, how to learn. We spent more time on that in our meetings than about doing the business.

I focused on helping my guys think about how we should live and be. I trusted them to get the daily work of the business done."

Retaining the right people has become central for Jay. "I have a business philosophy: It doesn't matter how great an idea you have, or how good a process, or how much money. If you don't have the right people, you won't win the game. It's so hard to get the right people. It's not 80/20, it's 90/10. It's egregious to lose a great person because it's so hard to find them. Each person on the margin that you don't lose is someone who helps you. I've always wanted to build the company in such a way that no one wants to leave. It should be a place where they're happy. If that's true, and they're making the right money, they won't take calls from recruiters trying to tempt them away."

BOTTOM LINE

1. Culture is neither good nor bad. It simply is.

2. Culture is defined by, and flows from, the founders. Live, breathe, and embody those behaviors. Codify them, yes, and put them on the wall, but spread them through your own day-to-day choices.

3. Culture has to be intentional, and it must transcend a single era of leadership. You need to be able to "teach your culture" through storytelling and historical examples of how the business was built and how it reached its current state.

4. The business world has changed. Power has shifted from employers to employees.

5. Potential hires are making decisions based on factors other than salary. Many of them are now looking for a cause to belong to, a fight to join, and a firm that's on a journey that they support.

6. To attract potential employees, focus on being and not on saying. Companies must now embody and foster their values, explicitly and publicly. And if they don't, word will get around faster than ever before.

7. Being authentic and consistent is more important than being interesting. Your authenticity will attract people who want to live and work in that way. Stick to your beliefs and trust they'll see you through. Ignore the doubters, who are generally short-termist liars.

8. Go beyond core values. Hire the right mindset to succeed.

9. People leave people, not companies. Have crucial conversations early—"eat the baby elephant before they grow into a large seven-ton elephant!"—to head off personnel disputes.

CHAPTER 10

BUILD A STRONG PEOPLE ECOSYSTEM

"In looking for people to hire, look for three qualities:
integrity, intelligence and energy. And if they don't
have the first, the other two will kill you."

–WARREN BUFFET

"Dad, I can't wait for you to meet Jack and Joan." (I'll be using pseudonyms to protect the guilty and the innocent.) "They're my two new VPs."

Ever since I'd started working in the United States, my parents and I had visited every year or two. Either I went back to Singapore or they came to visit me. "They are really smart," I told my dad, "and I am thrilled I was able to recruit them to join my company."

Dad met my two new VPs, and then two years later, my parents visited me again. "You know, I'm looking forward to seeing Jack and Joan again," my father said.

"Oh, Jack and Joan. Hmm. Well," I had to tell him, "not this year, Dad. Things with them didn't go so well, and they're not with me anymore."

"Why? What happened? I thought you said they were really smart?" my father asked, concerned.

"Oh, don't worry about it. Sure, when they first got here, they were great. But after two years, they could not keep up," I explained, "so I guess they turned out to be pretty dumb, after all."

My father paused thoughtfully and then said, "Son, I have an observation. Would you like to hear it?" I don't know about you, but I hate it when my dad tells me he has "an observation." It tends to mean that I've missed something obvious. "Sure, Dad, please share your observation," I said, and braced myself to learn about something I'd missed.

"My observation is that smart people come to work for you, and in two years ... they become dumb!" Before I could refute his finding, he said something else that really pierced my heart: "What part do you play in that?"

I had failed Jack and Joan as their CEO. I had failed as their leader. It is painful and expensive when people leave the company. Their knowledge, the relationships they left with—these are all the investments I had made and lost. It was expensive to recover from losing them on many fronts: financially, culturally (their firings had created negative energy), opportunity-wise, and time-wise—and as we know, time in early stage, high-growth companies is critical. Finally, the emotional toll on me as well as their team members when they left was heavy. I was being flippant when I said they were "dumb." Of course, they were not dumb. It was my way of deflecting the pain I felt when their names were brought up. Over the last two years, we had gotten to know one another well while working together. They were my friends too, and I felt betrayed that they had left. But I had not thought that I had failed them. That realization was the gift my father gave me that day.

It is my job as a leader to help my team members grow. I sucked. I had to de-suck myself.

IT IS MY JOB AS A LEADER TO HELP MY TEAM MEMBERS GROW. I SUCKED. I HAD TO DE-SUCK MYSELF.

THE POWER OF HAVING THE RIGHT PEOPLE AROUND YOU

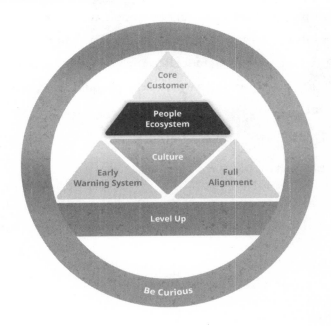

Great execution comes from having great focus, alignment, and accountability to achieve your commitments. The work is done by people. If your team is not well led or equipped with the right skills, then you are already failing right out of the gate! When your team is well led and well equipped, commitments get achieved with less stress and drama. Life is good!

On the flip side, when your people are not up to the task, there is much drama and emotional pain. The work just seems harder. Life sucks!

The difference is people. This chapter will explore why it is important to prioritize having the right team in place. Most companies make the mistake of prioritizing team improvements *after* important work. That's like choosing to chop wood with a blunt ax. It is going to take more energy and time, and you will end up chopping less wood. Instead, you should stop chopping wood and take the time to sharpen your ax. You might be slower to start, but you will have more output and end up with more chopped wood.

Choosing work over working on people will burn more energy, resources, and time and result in less output. You will be fooled, thinking you are producing more because you will be working harder to get things done. Working harder does not equal better results. This chapter will focus on:

1. building the right organization and
2. renewing to keep the right organization.

We will then explore other critical components of your people ecosystem that also have an important impact on your journey to success:

3. Investors and board members
4. Coaches

THE REAL COST OF GETTING PEOPLE DECISIONS WRONG

If you choose to prioritize the hard work of getting the right team in place and keeping them strong, you will be on a more joyful journey to success. If you do not make this choice, you will experience a more painful and tiring journey. There is real cost in not doing this hard work.

The Negative Impact of a Poor Leader

Companies outgrow leaders. This is an unfortunate situation that you will have to address repeatedly as your company grows. You must level up and so must your leaders. It is your job to help your leaders grow, and it is their job to grow. You cannot force them to develop no matter how hard you try. A pattern of failure I have noticed is when leaders put more effort into their team members' growth than the team members put themselves.

MICHAEL'S PERSPECTIVE

We had a senior leader at AvidXchange who needed to improve his communication and follow-through. This gap was causing miscommunication, delays, and rework. He had great ideas that did not result in good execution. He frustrated many of his peers and his own team. I decided to invest in him by providing an executive coach. Week after week, he did not make time to contact the list of coaches we provided for him so that he could interview them and begin a coaching program. This is a good example of me caring more than he did about his development. Maybe he thought he was better in this area than we did. Maybe he did not feel the same sense of urgency to improve. It doesn't really matter why. What was important is that we were willing to invest in his growth, but he was not taking the initiative. After a month of reminding him to interview coaches, we decided we could no longer wait for him to invest time in himself. We had to move on from him. It was a tough decision, but I have learned that a poor leader has a cascading negative effect on their peers, the team that works for them, and the opportunity cost that extends to customers and projects.

It's really a disservice to the people who work for a poor leader if we do not address the issue. The leader needs to work on leveling up, or we need to make a change.

In the past, I tended to wait too long to make a change. I convinced myself that I had to give the person more time. Over time, I began to realize that more time without a clear plan of improvement with the right actions only delayed the inevitable. More time did not give us successful outcomes. In fact, more time only frustrated employees and hurt customer projects. We lost some great talent along the way because top talent chose not to suffer under poor leaders for long.

We had successful outcomes only when the leader in question took feedback to heart and made self-improvement a priority. When this happens, we have a good chance of succeeding. I have learned that I can provide the observations or feedback and invest the resources for growth, but it is the leader who has to choose to level up. I don't have the power to level them up.

Many of us do not pause to calculate the cumulative negative impact and costs of a poor leader. Our compassion and empathy for the leader in question may blind us to the cascading negative effects down the line. Keeping leaders in management positions who leave a trail of negative energy is like burning your monthly payroll dollars.

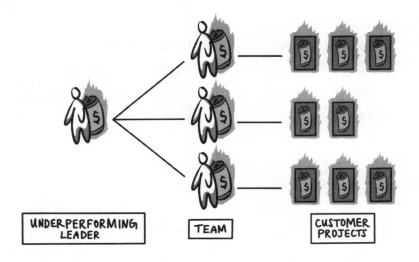

Think about your monthly payroll. Your ROP is the productivity of your employees on payroll. Since payroll is a fixed cost, if productivity goes up, then your ROP increases. If your productivity goes down, then your ROP drops. By definition, an underperforming leader is delivering less than expected, so their ROP is lower than expected. Even while reading this book, you have underperforming leaders. You are burning payroll dollars.

Employees reporting to underperforming leaders are not getting the inspiration and instruction they require to perform well. Their ROP also drops because of poor leadership from their underperforming leader. Poor leadership may stifle innovation and create an environment that discourages team members from seizing opportunities or trying new things. You are burning more payroll dollars.

Finally, customers who are being managed by these employees may be receiving slower service or late delivery because of poor leadership from above. Projects may be delayed, and customers might leave you. You are burning even more payroll dollars.

And that's the negative impact of an underperforming leader on your organization.

This is both an opportunity to build a great company and a pit of quicksand that senior leaders fall into. You can provide your leaders with growth and development opportunities as long as they take these to heart and take the initiative to improve themselves within an agreed-upon timeline. The choice is yours, but I believe you should have the courage to extinguish your burning dollars.

Dr. Jay Cohen was the CEO of Signature Consultants until he successfully merged his staffing company with DISYS to create Dexian, a billion-dollar company. Jay shared with me that he had to learn the hard way that leaders who have poor emotional intelligence, especially those who lack empathy, did not deliver strong results as managers. During his long and successful career, when he was faced with such situations, he would value that leader's individual skills and contributions and quickly move them to an individual contributor role. He learned that they were unable to inspire the team members they led.

I noticed the same pattern. I often promoted people who were very good at their jobs into leadership roles. Unfortunately, some of them did not have the emotional intelligence to see or sense the effect they had on the people they led. I wish I had learned this lesson faster and acted quicker as Dr. Jay did.

The Emotional Impact

Solving people problems is challenging and may be emotionally draining. Your ability to reach a resolution depends heavily on the relationship that you have built with the employee. Michael, for example, likes to spend focused one-on-one time with all of his key leaders outside of the office environment over breakfasts, lunches, and dinners in order to be both fully present and to be able to connect with his team on a more personal level. Michael finds that having these deeper connections pays dividends when trying to navigate future roles and organizational changes. He is depositing into their emotional bank accounts.

A CEO said to me, "My chief operating officer (COO) is falling behind. I've been friends with Frank forever, and he's been at the firm almost as long as I have. I really don't want to fire him, but it's too late to develop him." Then came a rhetorical question: "Why didn't I bite the bullet and just fire Frank two years ago?" I hear this a lot. Even if someone is tough to work with, the bonds of shared history will always influence our choices. This is a tough and unpalatable decision to make. Overly focusing on the underperforming individual is a mistake that blinds us to the multiple issues that are developing as time goes by. What this CEO did not take into account was that he had been doing part of his COO's job, leading to his own overwork, stress, and underperformance. Burning payroll extended up to the CEO as well!

Personnel Issues Take a Toll on Mental and Physical Health

Personnel issues often bring a tremendous level of stress. One of my clients, Jack, was dealing with the stress of working with his business partner.

Jack noticed a change in his breathing during his regular runs. Concerned, he checked in with his doctor. The tests came back showing his heart had developed an irregular rhythm. Fortunately, it was not atrial fibrillation (AFib), which can be life threatening, but it was still worrisome. He mentioned this to me during a coaching session.

"What do you think could be causing this irregular heart rhythm?" I asked, worried for him. "What about stress? I learned about how stress affects us physically and medically in unsuspecting ways. And since we cannot see stress, we usually do not think of it as a factor."

"I don't know," he pondered. "That is an interesting thought. Running a company does come with stress anyway. However, it has been really stressful trying to figure out stuff with my business partner for the last two years since our growth and profit started falling."

"I'll think more about that," he told me. I thought stress might be a contributing factor because Jack and his partner had been close friends before going into business together, and they had enjoyed working with each other for many years. However, the last few years had been tough as the company started doing poorly, and their opinions and ideas about how to solve problems started diverging. Jack believed that he had to choose between saving the company and his friendship with his business partner. His business partner believed that they could still solve their business problems together. Jack left our coaching session with a lot to process.

Jack reached a decision the next month. "We're going to go our separate ways," Jack said. Jack was sad but shared that once his partner agreed to move on from the business, he felt a weight lifted off his shoulders. He was hoping that their friendship would survive this event. "Time heals all wounds, right?" He gave a rueful smile.

Over the next two months, Jack's heart rhythm returned to normal, and years later, the irregularities haven't returned.

What about Loyalty?

MICHAEL'S PERSPECTIVE

I believe that people who have helped me grow AvidXchange to this point of success should have the opportunity to grow and develop themselves. I spend a lot of time trying to help people through their skills and leadership gaps. Previously, I allowed too much time to pass, and I did not hold them accountable to a timeline. But after getting large investors, the time tolerance for improvement has shrunk down. My investors have put in serious money, and they are not waiting around. They want to see meaningful movement and positive change. Many entrepreneurs who have attached large rounds of funding might not realize that with the funding comes an expectation of moving faster with solving people issues.

I've been accused of being too loyal and giving people too many chances and too much time to develop themselves. While I am a loyal person, it's also more about their value to the company. AvidXchange is very complex. If I lose five people, I can't replace them without a lot of catching up with AvidXchange's domain knowledge, which tends to lead to delay and expense. AvidXchange is growing fast, and the payment system is complicated, with billions of dollars and millions of vendors. Trust is vital, and we can't afford to screw anything up. Our existing people get that, and that lets them make better decisions.

I believe that giving people the opportunity to develop themselves is the right thing to do for the company and for the individual who needs to grow. If I give someone a chance and it doesn't work out, I'll have no problem replacing them.

I have also been fortunate to have chosen the right investors and board members. They have seen a lot, have patterns of success, and are fast to give me feedback. These investors and board members really helped me mature from a startup CEO to a public company CEO.

BUILDING THE RIGHT ORGANIZATION

Many leaders will say that their people are their most important assets. But is this true for you? Are your people the wind behind your sails or the anchors around your neck? They are not automatically assets. It takes intentional work to recruit and develop A-Players. C-Players may actually be sucking your energy and dragging your company down.

Build an Organization of A-Players

In his book *Good to Great*, Jim Collins teaches that we should make sure we have the right people in our company and in the right job roles.

I want to help you focus on making sure that you have A-Players and not C-Players in your company. Let's get more wind behind your sails and free you from the anchors around your neck!

Jack Welch (the famous former CEO of General Electric) shared a four-box model to assess employee performance in his book *Winning*. The key lesson is to assess an employee's performance on two axes: (1) measurable results and outcomes and (2) culture and core values. It is not enough to only deliver strong results. To be an A-Player, the employee must also work well with others in the company. They should be adding joy and energy to other team members and not depleting their energy. A-Players are those who deliver good results and are also multipliers who help others grow stronger as a team. They know how to achieve results in a way that also enables others to succeed. They put the team ahead of themselves.

D	A
STRONG RESULTS POOR VALUES	STRONG RESULTS STRONG VALUES
C	B
POOR RESULTS POOR VALUES	POOR RESULTS STRONG VALUES

Here is my take on the four-box model. The top-right box contains your A-Players. They are giving you great results and are demonstrating a strong culture fit. They are living the company's core values and are a joy to work with.

At the bottom right are your B-Players. They are not giving you good results, but they are a good culture fit. These people might be the right people on the bus, but they're in the wrong seat. They may have the wrong job or may need training to do their job well.

The bottom-left box contains your C-Players. They are producing poor results and are a poor culture fit. You should graciously let these people go and free up their futures so that they can be great somewhere else. I do believe that everyone can be an A-Player at the right company. These folks might just be trying hard at the wrong company for them. And if they aren't trying hard to improve, then you don't want them messing up your company anyway.

At the top left are your D-Players. They are producing good, maybe even great results, but are a poor culture fit. They are hard to work with, and these good results are coming at the cost of screwing up your culture and company environment. We are tempted to tolerate their behavior and even make excuses on their behalf. Every time you make an exception for D-Players, you are sending the message to the rest of the company that your core values and culture do not apply as long as results are being delivered. These fast, short-term results come at the cost of building the team and company culture you desire to take your company further. You can go faster for a short while with a D-Player or go much further with a great team.

YOU CAN GO FASTER FOR A SHORT WHILE WITH A D-PLAYER OR GO MUCH FURTHER WITH A GREAT TEAM.

Working with D-Players is hard; I empathize because I have done it in my own companies. None of us are immune to having C- and D-Players on our teams. Even with experience, it does not get any easier. I had a sales executive—let's call him Jack—who achieved his sales quota and much more. However, he was hard to work with, had very little appreciation for his teammates, and violated our core values repeatedly, especially under pressure. He enjoyed our company culture; he just was not able to live our culture.

"But he is doing so well in sales!" I whined to my executive team who were holding me accountable to getting Jack to change his behavior or to let him go. So I worked hard coaching Jack. I educated him repeatedly on behavior that would be consistent with our core values. I also educated him on how we measure performance, not just based on outcomes but also with equal weight on behavior. I did not mince my words, sharing with him that he was in the D-Player quadrant and that he would either have to work with the team according to our values or he would be managed out of the company.

Even though I had warned him repeatedly that he was not performing well, Jack actually asked for a raise, because he had exceeded his sales quota. Regardless of my coaching on the importance of our core values, Jack valued his performance only on one axis: the vertical axis of results! He did not make it. When I finally asked him to leave the company, he was surprised. It just did not register in his mind that our company culture and values were just as important to our company as the work results. An A-Player delivers results in a stress-free way. A D-Player achieves outcomes through methods fraught with stress, akin to the disruptive impact a tornado would have on your company's culture.

I want to inspire you to build a company of A-Players. If you have C-Players and D-Players in your company, you are wasting so much energy on managing the drama coming from their disruptive behavior. And if you have C-Players, what are you waiting for? They are not performing, and they are being disruptive to your team and culture while you are paying them. Your ROP is poor!

You will get what you tolerate. If you tolerate team members who don't pay attention to your core values, then you will have a company of people who do not live by your values. If you choose to take action and coach them to either become A-Players or facilitate their exit from your company, you will end up with more A-Players in your company who will become the wind behind your sails.

YOU WILL GET WHAT YOU TOLERATE. IF YOU TOLERATE TEAM MEMBERS WHO DON'T PAY ATTENTION TO YOUR CORE VALUES, THEN YOU WILL HAVE A COMPANY OF PEOPLE WHO DO NOT LIVE BY YOUR VALUES.

Jeff Berstein was the CEO of ImageFIRST when we discussed the importance of developing more A-Players in his company. Image-FIRST is one of the largest and fastest-growing companies providing laundry services to the healthcare industry. Inspired, Jeff set the goal of having A-Players comprise 70 percent of his workforce. His HR team defined the boxes with clear criteria for all the different jobs and assessed his associates, letting each associate flow naturally into one of the four. He then asked each manager to provide a plan that would help their people move into the A-box within one or two quarters.

On the first assessment, only 30 percent of ImageFIRST's employees qualified as A-Players. After a couple of quarters, this had risen to 42 percent, which was encouraging, but the number didn't continue to trend upward. I looked at his exercise and saw that around 40 percent of his managers occupied the A-box. "Let's take a different route," I suggested. "What if we focused on developing your managers into great managers? What if we were able to raise the bar for managers and get 70 percent of them to develop into A-Player managers? Then these good managers will do their jobs and might solve the problem of developing associates who are A-Players as well."

We redirected our efforts toward transforming managers into top performers, which yielded impressive outcomes. Within two quarters, Jeff saw 70 percent of his managers reach A-Player performance. Remarkably, these managers also actively coached their team members, leading to a ripple effect. Consequently, in the same time frame, Jeff accomplished his objective of elevating 70 percent of all associates to A-Player status!

Focusing on developing managers into A-Players had a multiplier effect. Many of the managers rose to the challenge and developed their leadership abilities. In turn, these talented managers led their people well, helped them to grow, and inspired them to deliver strong results and to embody ImageFIRST's core values. Jeff put it succinctly: "As go the leaders, so go their teams."

Invest in Your A-Players First

Years ago, I recall walking unannounced into one of my programmers' cubicles. This surprised him, and he immediately freaked out. "Why are you here? What did I screw up? If you're here, I must have screwed up royally!"

"You're a high performer," I told him. "I'm interested in what you're doing. I want to spend time with the best people." I went on to have a wonderful working session and learned a lot from him.

"Patrick, that was pretty fun," he said. "I hope you come by again." That working session encouraged a very talented team member and changed his expectations about how I spend my time. I then asked myself, "What am I doing wrong so that my employees automatically believed that only mistakes and poor performance deserved my attention?" I realized that I had to change my own behavior and how I related to my team members. I had to let them know through my daily actions that I wanted to devote more time and energy to high-performing team members.

In numerous organizations, sales team leaders concentrate on underperforming members, aiming to enhance their performance. However, this approach can be flawed, as typically, 80 percent of a company's business is generated by its top performers. Therefore, leaders should primarily focus their efforts on these individuals. This isn't to say that leaders shouldn't support their struggling team members—they certainly should. However, a larger share of their attention should be dedicated to their best performers and coaching them to further excel. The most significant portion of a leader's time should be invested in further developing their A-Players.

RENEWING TO KEEP THE RIGHT ORGANIZATION

Develop Your Future Organization

The challenges of working in a growth company increase over time. Complexity and difficulty both rise as the business develops. Your people need to keep up, whether that means adapting to new competition, adopting new technology, or just grappling with the growing size of their portfolio and team. Being able to visualize and articulate the future and evangelize your people into this vision is a key step in helping them prepare for these challenges.

To succeed, you need to keep one foot in the present and the other foot in the future!

You are already in the present, so let's get your other foot into the future. First, craft a clear vision of your company's future state, envisioning a time frame of one or two years ahead. Paint a picture of your future, including details such as the following:

1. *Customer Growth*: Imagine which of your current customers have evolved and expanded alongside your company.

2. *Product and Service Portfolio*: Will your products and services become more diverse or more focused? Are there new products and services that you intend to offer? How will you introduce, market, and sell these new products?

3. *Financial Targets*: What will your financial profile look like? What will your revenue and profits be? What key metrics will you use to measure and track your journey?

YOU NEED TO KEEP ONE FOOT IN THE PRESENT AND THE OTHER FOOT IN THE FUTURE!

Next, envision a new organization to support this future company, as if conjured by a magic wand. In essence, consider how the future organization could be unencumbered by the constraints of your current organizational structure or team members. A common error is to formulate future organizational structures with the existing personnel in mind, which tends to constrain imaginative thinking and curtail overall growth potential. It's time to wield that figurative magic wand! Visualize your future organization chart, and populate it with the ideal skills and anticipated outcomes for each role or position within the chart. Let your aspirations guide you as you craft this transformative blueprint for your organization's future. Your blueprint should include the following details for each role or position:

1. Purpose of the role
2. Description of the role
3. Skills required to succeed in this role
4. Results and outcomes expected from this role

Now you are ready to fill the roles and design growth opportunities for your team members. Each role can be filled by a new hire or by existing team members. Start with your executive team. For each person, consider which roles they might do well in. Yes, you may consider a person for multiple roles! Compare their current skills to the list of skills and competencies that you have already written down. For each role, is there a gap in skill or experience that the candidate needs to fill?

This exercise can be a positive experience for every team member. When you map current employees to future roles, you will find gaps in skills required to succeed in the new role. These gaps represent opportunities for every individual to level up as the company grows. Avoid the pitfall of having a negative conversation: "Here are five ways you aren't doing well right now." Instead, you can help them paint a successful picture of their future selves at work: "We are creating a terrific future together. I want to help you plan your career growth path to take advantage of new opportunities that come about due to our company's successful growth."

This exercise creates space for you to explore multiple roles for current team members. Encourage your team members to take some time and explore different roles. Use this opportunity to solve difficult organizational challenges. For example, a leader who runs operations today might not be the right fit to run operations for a larger company.

However, they might do very well and experience growth running the new customer success team.

As your company grows, new leadership roles will be naturally created. These new roles will provide career opportunities for many team members to explore if they are prepared with the necessary job and leadership skills to succeed in these new roles. Don't fall into the trap of thinking narrowly about titles. Today's operations manager does not have to be tomorrow's COO. If they do not have the skills to succeed or the potential and desire to grow the necessary skills, it does not serve either the individual or the company to promote them into roles in which they cannot succeed. Promote them into a different role where they can grow and thrive.

There is power and momentum in having the right employees around you. Just as there was joy, excitement, pain, and clumsiness when you were growing up as a child, you should expect the same when growing your business. This future organization exercise will help you to make it routine to choose the right people and help them get into the right seats to make them, and your company, successful. Outgrowing some team members is inevitable when you grow a company. The question is not whether your company will outgrow existing employees; the question is, how do you proactively plan for such events and help your employees grow with your firm and continue to be part of your journey?

Ultimately, it's the CEO who has to pick up the slack. They'll do the job of a failing executive because there's no one else who can, and this distraction can compromise the CEO's own role.

Retaining and developing great talent are necessary for every growing company. If you do not get this right, you will fail. Great people want great career opportunities and will be excited to grow and stretch to meet the challenges and opportunities ahead. The chances of retention are boosted by providing employees with a growth plan. People also respond well when change is done in a respectful way. If you wish to go far and win with your current team, you will need to be intentional about prioritizing and dedicating resources to help them grow. You will need their inspired participation in the company's future.

MICHAEL'S PERSPECTIVE

Patrick reminds me to review my talent and organization on a regular basis using these tools. During one of our sessions, as I reflected on my organization for the future, I realized that our chief technology officer (CTO) was being stretched in too many directions. He had responsibility for product development, internal infrastructure, and PC support. Patrick suggested that I take my eyes off my CTO and focus on building the future organization without this concern.

When we finished the organizational structure and role definitions, the CTO's current role had grown into three distinct roles on the future organization chart. I could not see him wearing all three hats, so I decided to meet with him and discuss our future growth and organizational needs. I got myself ready for a difficult conversation. Then I realized that I was making it harder by thinking of this in a negative way–that he had to give up part of his current role. Instead, I should be having a positive conversation about the future, growth opportunities, and exploring what he really enjoyed doing.

"Look, you're wearing three hats right now. Which do you like the most, and which do you dislike? Because as we achieve our growth targets, I can hire someone else to take the responsibilities you don't love. And if we keep doing that, over time, you'll be left only with the work you most enjoy." Our CTO shared that he really did not enjoy PC support and would gladly relinquish that to focus on product development as soon as the company was able to afford additional resources. What he most enjoyed was developing code, something I wouldn't have known unless we had this conversation about growing into our future together.

Working with a coach or an advisor can be especially helpful here. It is very hard to brainstorm by yourself or even with your executive team. A coach can bring a neutral perspective and provide patterns and examples that have been proven to work at other companies.

A coach can also help you assess your current leaders. Can this leader do that future job? What are their skill gaps or leadership gaps for the roles that are being considered? Help them develop a clear path of growth, and equip them to meet the new challenge.

I did this future organization exercise every year in our early days, because AvidXchange was growing at 40–50 percent and doubling in size every two years. I believe in giving our existing employees growth opportunities as our company grows. This process has given me a regular cadence to think about how our employees can grow as our business grows.

I Have a Great Team

"I have a great team." It's something I hear all often, without the evidence to back up that statement. This is an emotional confirmation bias that most leaders have, especially if the team was the team that helped them grow the company to its current level of success. Of course, you believe your team is great. After all, you hired them. But that was yesterday. Have they been able to evolve and continue to be great in their roles as the company grows?

Piers Carey, CEO of Teneo, a global public relations and advisory firm, shared, "The people who got us to $30 million weren't the people to get us to $60 million. We'd gone through a big growth spurt, and through the coaching I'd received, I knew I had to make sure I was working with the right employees to get the job done. 'Right people, right seat'—that was the mantra. And so, I had to say to some people, 'You're a good person for your role now, but you won't be the right person two years from now.'"

Step away from the daily operations, and adopt an objective perspective. It's not about making personnel changes; instead, it's about creating avenues for new opportunities to be birthed. Michael, for instance, emphasizes the practice of conducting the future organization exercise annually as a means to unearth growth prospects for his team members. Michael's approach reflects a growth-oriented mindset, highlighting the commitment to fostering growth and opportunities within the organization.

It's crucial to acknowledge that with growth, the roles within your team will undergo significant changes in the future. Even if a thorough evaluation of your team triggers a moment of apprehension, and you think, "Oh crap, my team might not be up to the task," it's essential to recognize that this realization provides valuable insights and data for making informed decisions.

Removing Obstacles

As a company surpasses the capabilities of a senior leader, and their leadership deficiencies remain unaddressed, this individual can inadvertently impede progress for others. The higher the leader's position, the more resistant to change they may become. Consequently, instead of collaborating with such leaders, people begin to circumvent them, leading to the emergence of conflicts and disruptions. Despite pouring additional energy and resources into the situation, progress slows down because the leader has unwittingly evolved into a hindrance. They cease to be effective multipliers, and, since they lack the necessary skills, crucial projects passing through them experience delays and diminished quality. Over time, they transform into obstacles that sap the energy of other employees and diminish overall productivity.

Employees expect their senior leaders to remove obstacles from their path. It's your job to confront and remove these obstacles. Your employees do not have the ability or the authority to do so. And if you wait too long, the joy of working in your company will deteriorate, and you will probably lose some really good, talented employees.

Remove the obstacles. That's your job.

INVESTORS AND BOARD MEMBERS

Today Michael Praeger has a strong board and deep working relationships with each of his board members. When Bain Capital Ventures (BCV) first invested in AvidXchange, Matt Harris from BCV joined AvidXchange's board of directors. Mike and I discussed how to tap into Matt's insights and advice. "Why don't you get into a regular rhythm with Matt? How often do you think you would like to connect with him?"

Mike thought about it and shared, "I think chatting with Matt weekly will help me get to know him faster, give him the information he needs, and give me the opportunity to run key decisions by him. This will help me get a different perspective and more insights."

MICHAEL'S PERSPECTIVE

Founders and CEOs sometimes view their board members with caution and struggle with transparency for fear of appearing weak while soliciting advice. Instead, having the right board members with both experiences and skill sets that are different or more advanced than your own is a powerful growth lever. Rather than being threatened or believing that it will weaken how your board views you as the CEO of the business, allow yourself to experience the opposite. Great leaders have a curiosity factor and are continuous learners who take the vulnerable position of challenging themselves to see what they can learn from each board member. In building AvidXchange, I have gained an incredible amount of insights about leadership and how to scale a business to the next inflection point of growth from each of my board members over the years, including Matt Harris and Nigel Morris.

Choosing the right board members and investors makes a huge difference for any company. It's particularly critical for any high-growth business as the pace of key decisions is significantly more rapid and the ability to quickly tap into each of your board members for insights can determine your company's fate. Key investors can also serve a similar purpose. They don't just hold the CEO and company accountable to results. You share very aligned objectives, and the right investors for each stage of growth can pay dividends in sharing their experiences across multiple portfolio companies at similar stages. Over the years at AvidXchange, both my board members and investors have provided company-changing insights and relationships in the following areas:

- Sharing industry insights
- Creating strategic partnerships
- Accessing the next stage of capital
- Helping attract and recruit top talent
- Connecting me with fellow CEO peers who may be struggling with similar issues
- Providing outside perspectives and evaluation of senior leadership talent based on past experiences of seeing what growth and scale look like at similar companies

When you are experiencing difficulty and challenges, survival instinct rears its ugly head, and it is natural to get closed in. Instead, fight that instinct, and reach out to your board members and advisors early. That way you have more time and insights to help you create options to solve your challenges.

Mort O'Sullivan was the founder and CEO of ARCA. The company had enjoyed many years of wonderful growth. Then sales began to fall off, and they started missing their numbers as growth slowed down. Mort did just what Michael suggested: he turned to his board for advice and insights. One of his board members threw out the option of bringing in a turnaround consultant to assist Mort. Mort hesitated even though he thought it was a good idea. When I asked him why he was hesitating, he shared his fear: "Well, in most of these turnarounds, the CEO also gets fired. And in this case, that CEO would be me."

I suggested that Mort lean in and lean in hard! Instead of circling the wagons and doing it on his own, consider leading the process to find the right turnaround consultant to help change the company's negative financial trend. "If your board sees you proactively solving whatever problems your company has and that you're willing to seek help, that's a good thing. If you get defensive and resist, you might be replaced, or even worse, your company might die. So why not jump in and lead this process instead of being worried and concerned? After all, you already believe that it is the right thing to do."

That was a few years ago. Mort worked with the turnaround expert, saved his company, and continued to lead ARCA back to a growth path. He went on to achieve a positive sale of his company, making all his investors and himself successful and proud of their journey together.

I suspect that if Mort did not consider the suggestion of that board member, ARCA might not have succeeded at that crucial point in their journey. Listening and leaning into the advice from his investors, and having the opportunity to reflect on and discuss his situation, allowed Mort to see things from many different perspectives and act quickly and decisively.

COACHES

MICHAEL'S PERSPECTIVE

Taking AvidXchange from a startup in Charlotte, North Carolina, to its current status as a publicly traded company with nearly $400 million in revenue has been an exceptionally demanding journey. Serving as the founder CEO throughout this evolution has presented daily challenges. As long as AvidXchange continues to grow and succeed, I wake up every day running the biggest company I have ever run. It's a privilege to lead our journey. I don't want to get it wrong, yet, at the same time, I need to make decisions that might be wrong. Having coaches with unique experiences that are different from my own, who bring patterns of success from other companies, has been critical to making more right decisions than wrong decisions. The cost of a coach pales in comparison to the cost of making a poor decision. In addition, you need to have very strong chemistry and trust in the coaches you work with in order for you to be vulnerable and discuss anything you need to discuss.

The best athletes all have multiple coaches. Business is very similar to playing on a sports team, so it always made sense to me to have coaches in various parts of the business. This has allowed me to grow fast enough personally to keep pace with my company's fast growth. Coaching sessions force me to slow down and reflect on important business decisions before I actually make them. I call this "scrimmaging the play," just as a sports team would do before a big game in order to understand all aspects and dynamics of the decision from others who have different experience and skill levels. Patrick has created space for me in my work cadence to slow down and consider various angles, making sure we made the right major decisions in new product offerings and winning move strategies, helping me ensure our M&A opportunities are in line with our strategy, and evaluating top talent across the company.

Patrick and I have now worked together for over twenty-three years—ever since AvidXchange was just an idea. This would not have been possible without a deep level of trust, which has allowed us to have brutally honest discussions and curiously learn from each other.

Although Patrick has never run a business as large as AvidXchange, he has a super power of asking direct, tough questions along with the experience of seeing many other companies at different stages of growth navigate similar challenges.

Patrick has brought his experience to help me navigate talent decisions and get the right leaders in the right seats.

He has done this by helping me identify where one of my leaders who has been instrumental in building our business in the past is now struggling with their current role. These situations are incredibly hard to see at times as I have been in the trenches on the battlefield with this person for years, but Patrick brings a perspective of what the characteristics of a talented leader for the role should look like, which has helped me make difficult decisions to ensure we have the best talent for our current stage of growth.

The following are a couple of accounts from successful CEOs who utilized coaching to accelerate their success.

Sheldon Wolitski: A Lifetime of Coaching

Sheldon grew The Select Group (TSG), a technology staff augmentation firm, from startup to $200 million over twenty-five years. Coaching has been central to his success for many years. "What my coaches have helped me do is really lose the cape and really get more to my authentic self." Sheldon has benefited from a lifetime of coaching, beginning with his hockey career and continuing into his life as CEO of TSG. "People ask about the biggest piece of my success through turbulent times, and it was this: having a coach at my back. People also think of a coach as someone who pumps up your tires and gives you confidence, but a good coach exposes your blind spots, holds you accountable, and keeps you grounded."

That has turned out to be important as Sheldon interacts regularly with the media. "As a CEO, you're in the news, there's publicity, and everyone around you is telling you, 'You're the man!' But you need someone," he added, "to slap you around a little bit. That's had a huge impact personally. It's easy to let ego creep in, or to have 'yes people' around you, because you're at the top of the food chain. No one tells you 'no,' and that's what the coach is there for."

Coaching has been so important that when Sheldon moved on from his CEO role and became the executive chairman, he kept his coach. "I'll have him for the rest of my life, because it's so important to me. Top performers, whether they're CEOs or athletes, need this kind of support. Even when Tiger Woods was at his peak, he had *seven* coaches surrounding him."

The quality of coaching depends on your coach and on your willingness to listen and take their advice seriously. "I have vivid memories of those sessions with Patrick. He's like Yoda from Star Wars. He has this wealth of knowledge and information, and he just shoots straight. If you're not ready and don't have your armor on," Sheldon warned, "you won't be able to handle it. You need to be ready."

He's found that about 80 percent of people are receptive to coaching. "But there's always a minority who will be resistant to that kind of feedback. They don't want a coach or to be held accountable. That's unfortunate," he said, "because it's such a growth opportunity. The kind of person who'll refuse coaching will end up bouncing around between different companies and leadership positions, never staying anywhere for long."

Given his sports background and openness to learning, Sheldon was always going to seek out coaches from a broad range of disciplines. "You're either growing or you're dying," he often puts it. "As I started to evolve as a leader, I surrounded myself with peak performers in nutrition, health and wellness, longevity, and biohacking modalities," by which he meant exposure to extremes of heat and cold and very stressful physical and psychological situations. "I hired former military coaches to push me through the kind of experiences that the Special Forces go through. I was at my peak performance when they were there," he remembered, "but none of it had to do with running a company. It was about dealing with stress and uncomfortable situations, being vulnerable, getting the right food, and getting enough sleep."

Bob Potter: Deeply Experienced and Still Eager for Coaching

Coaching isn't just for new CEOs. Bob Potter has run and successfully exited multiple companies. He was already in his sixties and richly experienced as a business leader when I met him. "This is my last gig," he said when we partnered during his tenure as CEO of SentryOne. "Patrick, you have a reputation for helping CEOs succeed. I'd like you to do that for me. I want to invest in coaching and make sure my last CEO gig is as successful as possible. The cost of your coaching services is nothing compared to the cost of failure."

I admire Bob's humility and believe it's a quality that all seasoned CEOs should possess. Despite his wealth of experience, he understood that no CEO role comes with a guarantee of success. There always remains a possibility of failure, and it's imperative to make the right decisions and avoid pitfalls that can cause CEOs and companies to fail.

We reflected together on how coaching works. "Having someone to discuss things with, to zoom out and reflect with, is priceless," he told me. "It's also just good practice. It's not because I can't do the job. It's to help me crystallize what I know so I can take action faster." Bob and I had a wonderful coaching relationship as I walked with him on his journey through COVID-19 and, eventually, the very successful sale of SentryOne.

I believe everyone needs a coach. Even the great Steve Jobs of Apple had coaching from Bill Campbell. It does not matter how many times you have done the job. Every CEO job is unique and has great opportunities as well as obstacles to success. It takes a confident and humble leader to receive, enjoy, and benefit from coaching.

BOTTOM LINE

1. With great intention, your people can truly be your assets—the wind behind your sails instead of anchors around your neck.

2. The real cost of a poor leader is much greater than most people realize. Their negative impact cascades to the people whom they lead and the customers and projects that the whole team is working on.

3. Be aware of timely decision-making. There are hidden costs to not making a change when you should. Recognize the importance of biting the bullet and having that hard conversation when things truly aren't working out.

4. You will receive the performance you tolerate. If you tolerate B-Players, C-Players, and D-Players, you will receive the performance that they deliver.

5. Choose to focus and develop A-Player managers, and then allow these managers to develop their team members into A-Players.

6. Remove obstacles. Otherwise, drama is created, employees might get discouraged, and your best people might choose to move on.

7. The future organization exercise can be extremely powerful. Consider doing it once a year. Don't be afraid of change, and give people a chance when they show a willingness to grow.

8. Think of your investors as advisors. They are not your enemy. Ask what they want rather than guessing.

9. Get coaching. Multiple coaches can help you become the best possible corporate athlete.

10. A good coach will help you to see what you might not see. Taking action is up to you.

CHAPTER 11

FOCUS ON SERVING YOUR CORE CUSTOMER

"Your customers don't care about you. They don't care about
your product or service. They care about themselves, their
dreams, their goals. Now, they will care much more if you help
them reach their goals, and to do that, you must understand
their goals, as well as their needs and deepest desires."

–STEVE JOBS

WHY CAN'T I SELL MY STUFF?

Back in 1993, I had been trying to sell freight management software
to transportation managers and freight managers at large manufactur-
ers. I'd knocked on a lot of doors and given countless presentations.
Once a company's shipping gets past a certain shipping volume, it
becomes impossible for the transportation manager to calculate the

best decisions for every shipment. That's where our software became a very useful solution to save the company a bunch of money and to turn the transportation manager into a hero.

So, when TJX, the parent company of TJ Maxx, called me for a demo, I'd excitedly jumped on a plane. We put in a ton of effort, but it came to nothing. The same happened with Revlon and a depressing number of other potential clients. I had been doing this for more than a year, and I had sold nothing. Zip!

It did not make sense to me. If you were a large manufacturer that had a shipping bill over $40 million a year, we would save your company 5–15 percent of this large freight bill. That's over $2 million in savings a year! So we even had a great return on investment story. "We make transportation software," I said to myself. "That's what we do. We sell freight management systems. That means when we're trying to sell our product, we target either the transportation manager or the freight manager. Right?"

After more than a year of getting doors slammed in my face and talking to many friends and advisors, my team arrived at a logical conclusion: we must be selling to the wrong person.

Our team threw out what we believed about our core customer and went back to trying to answer the most basic question. Forget about job titles—who in a large manufacturing company would really care about our stuff? Whose life or job would really be much better? Who would embrace us? We arrived at a possible answer: "Someone willing to try something new to extract costs out of the supply chain and potentially save their company millions."

This person would have the following characteristics or needs:

1. They had to be willing to try new things—a visionary buyer.
2. They had to have the responsibility to reduce their company's supply chain costs. Even better if they had a mandate!
3. The company had to have a shipping budget of at least $40 million.

It turned out that their job title did not matter. In fact, we were fooled by selling to a job title instead of a real person. This person could be the head of supply chain or the head of distribution and logistics. Many of the freight managers did not want their jobs to change. In fact, many of them did not view our software as a way to become a hero; rather, they felt threatened by a system like ours that automated their jobs. And to top it all off, almost none of them had the mandate to extract cost savings from the supply chain.

This new thought turned out to be right! The person who held those three key characteristics (willingness to try new things, mandate, and budget) often turned out to be the VP of distribution or the VP of supply chain. Occasionally, the chief financial officer (CFO) had the power to make purchasing decisions at the right level—the mandate I needed them to have. But it was rarely the freight manager. I was calling the right companies but the wrong person.

The red herring was our belief that the freight and transportation manager was the right person who needed our product. Unfortunately, they were not looking for our solution. When we figured out who actually had the mandate to reduce cost in their supply chain regardless of their title, we discovered our true core customer. And the day we started focusing on making that core customer successful was the day that our company turned around. We experienced rocketing sales and achieved the rank of 151 on the Inc. 500 list in 1996.

KEY LESSONS ABOUT YOUR CORE CUSTOMER

Who Is Your Core Customer?

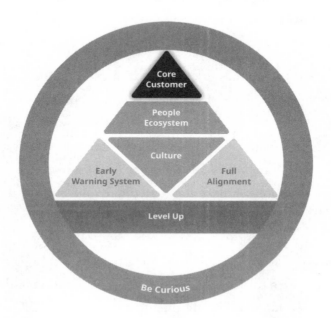

To play off George Orwell: All customers are created equal, but some customers are more equal than others. Your core customer is the most important customer you have. This final chapter is about designing and fine-tuning your strategy to serve your core customer.

ALL CUSTOMERS ARE CREATED EQUAL, BUT SOME CUSTOMERS ARE MORE EQUAL THAN OTHERS.

Peter Drucker says your primary customer is "One who values your service, who wants what you offer, who feels it's important to them." According to Drucker, it's important to design your entire company around this primary customer.

Many of us make the mistake of trying to please too many different types of customers. This leads us to build more complex services and products. In this case, you really do not want to be an all-purpose Swiss Army Knife. Instead, you want to figure out who truly needs your products or services. This is your core customer.

You make a real difference in this person's life because of your offerings. In my keynotes and workshops, when I ask people who their customers are, I often get answers like, "A professional female, between the ages of thirty-five and fifty," or, "Mid-market companies in the high technology industry." But these are examples of market segments. These are not descriptions of real people. Whether you are in a B2C (business-to-consumer) or B2B (business-to-business) company, we are all in the P2P (people-to-people) business. We serve people. To truly understand whom you serve, you need to go beyond the market segment definition. People buy from people. Your core customer is a person with real needs, real likes and dislikes, and real fears and concerns.

This chapter will discuss how important it is to design your strategy and position your offerings to the needs of your core customer and forget about the rest. If you can do this, your company will become very focused, and your products and services will be less complex and less expensive to maintain.

Your core customer should help you decide if your offering succeeds or fails in its intended use. This is the person your products and services need to delight. It's someone who allows you to have a profitable and thriving business today and grow with tomorrow. It is someone for whom you can continue to build products and services in the future.

Your core customer will fit the following descriptions:

- They are a good fit for your products and services today.
- They also provide a road map for you to build a successful business for the future.
- Because of the good product fit, they are easy to serve without much friction.
- Because of the good product fit, your team typically enjoys providing for these customers. Your team feels fulfilled as they are also living their purpose when servicing these customers.
- They need you. Your offerings fall into the category of "must have" and not "nice to have." They would miss you if you did not exist.

Your core customer definition should be short, no more than twenty-five words. Avoid corporate jargon. Make it simple, easy to read, and understandable, and then communicate it to everyone in your company. If you have to read it off a sheet in order to remember it, then you've already messed up.

For example, at Metasys, our core customer turned out to be "someone willing to try something new to extract savings from the supply chain of a company spending $40 million or more a year on shipping."

Your core customer definition should describe a person, not a market segment, and it should share what they need—maybe even what they are worried about.

Beyond Sales and Marketing

Defining your core customer is not only a sales and marketing opportunity. Your core customer should be the central obsession of all your employees. You should be building products and services that this customer needs. Your entire product, customer journey, and experience should be designed for this core customer.

YOUR ENTIRE PRODUCT, CUSTOMER JOURNEY, AND EXPERIENCE SHOULD BE DESIGNED FOR THIS CORE CUSTOMER.

Position strategically for your core customer, and sell tactically to others.

I often get the question "What if we have more than one core customer? We sell to many different customers." That might be true. However, if you push on this question harder, you might discover that these different customers have similar needs. If you can get down to a single core customer definition, this will significantly simplify your company products, offerings, and customer journey.

For example, Steve Jobs said that Apple stood at the intersection of technology and liberal arts. I believe Apple focuses on a core customer *who wants intuitive and beautifully designed technology products that just work and is willing to pay a premium price for such products*. I am an Apple core customer. Transcending both B2C and B2B, I am a person who enjoys the design, quality, and ease of use of Apple's products, and

I buy them in all parts of my life, both personal and professional. My friends laugh at me when I say that I would like to just give Apple my Amex card and have them bill and ship me their new products once they get released. As a tech geek, I buy them for myself. As a father, I buy them for my family (yes, we have a 100 percent Apple ecosystem in our home). And as a CEO, I buy them for my company.

Effectiveness requires focus. And there is no greater focus than to focus on ONE. It is tempting to believe that we have more than one core customer. Here are the typical reasons I have encountered that tempt us to design for more than one core customer:

1. We have different market segments that we sell to.
2. Our business has too many different products, so we require different core customers for different products.
3. We need more than one core customer to expand our market.

I have found that our most successful and happy customers have similar characteristics and needs, even if they were found in different market segments. When you distill it down to the most important characteristics, it is surprising how often the exercise ends up yielding one single core customer definition. If you can get down to this definition, your efforts—from product development to sales to implementation across your entire customer journey—will be easier, more focused, and more successful.

Focusing on a core customer requires a mindset shift. Focus means choosing to give time and energy to one set of customers and prospects and abandoning other prospects. Apple has demonstrated this practice repeatedly. They do not wish to sell their products to everyone—they focus on marketing to their core customers. Of course, anyone can purchase their products, but their products are designed and priced for their core customers. By shifting their mindset to focus on and design for a smaller set of customers versus the whole world, Apple has achieved continuous growth and profits year after year.

At the time of writing, Apple continues to be the most valuable company in the world. They sell to both consumers and businesses. They cross different industries, including computer hardware, software, mobile devices, wearables, music, payments, and video-streaming services. But still, they can define and focus on a single core customer. Can we not challenge ourselves to find that same focus and discover our single core customer?

CASE STUDIES

Identifying and committing to your core customer are transformational for your business, but it is not an instinctual process for most. To do this, you have to let go of your tightly held misconceptions and biases. You also have to improve your listening skills. Veeam, BioPlus, and AvidXchange have all undertaken this challenge. They have experienced the powerful impact of building a business around the core customer.

One Core Customer across Multiple Market Segments (Veeam Software)

I started working with Ratmir when Veeam just passed $100 million in revenues. Veeam provided solutions for backing up and replicating data across virtual machines to ensure data safety and recovery in case of data loss. If a company was running VMWare, Veeam was the perfect solution to back up their virtual machines.

We worked on Veeam's core customer definition in one of our early strategic planning sessions. They did not use this concept at that time. Instead, they defined market segments that they sold to and pursued all segments of the market according to this definition:

1. Single entrepreneurs (or companies with just two employees)
2. Small companies with less than twenty people
3. Small and medium businesses (SMBs)
4. Mid-market businesses
5. Small enterprises
6. Large enterprises

They were doing well with most of their customers in the small and SMB segments. They had happy and unhappy customers in all these segments, but they did have more unhappy customers as they progressed up the segments to larger enterprises.

I asked them to describe their best customer, not as a segment but as a person. I also asked them to describe their most difficult customers, those who needed a lot of resources and were harder to satisfy. This didn't happen instantly, of course. It took a couple of strategic planning sessions and some deeply facilitated discussions.

Our breakthrough came when we drew the market segments on the board and plotted where they had successful customers. We discussed and distilled what made these customers successful and how Veeam employees served them. We then plotted unsuccessful customers on these segments. We noticed that they had successful customers in every market segment. When we asked more questions about why they were successful, they came up with their core customer definition:

AN IT PROFESSIONAL WHO LOVES VIRTUALIZATION, IS WILLING TO CHANGE CURRENT PROCESSES, AND DESIRES PEACE OF MIND AND TO SLEEP WELL AT NIGHT.

They noticed that this person could be found in all of their customer segments. Then they noticed that when they were able to sell and serve this person in small and large enterprises, they were successful. Conversely, when they sold to someone with different needs, they had more issues and failures, even in the small and SMB segments within which they were usually very successful.

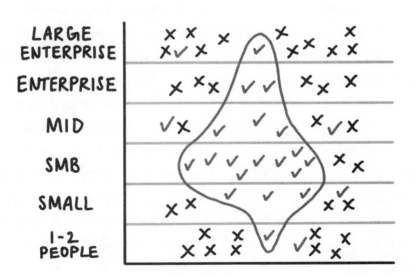

This turned out to be a very useful analysis. Veeam was having more successes (√) in the mid-market and SMB segments, but there were also unhappy customers (X). The diagram spurred a dialogue that helped define successful customers (whom Veeam was servicing happily and with whom there are few support calls) and unsuccessful customers (who are perhaps twice as expensive to service). Ratmir characterized the difference between the two as the level of friction Veeam experienced when dealing with them. Low-friction customers yielded fewer phone calls, better margins, a lower cost of service, and a higher happiness level. As you'd expect, high-friction customers required more energy and resources, all while showing signs that they might leave Veeam and buy elsewhere.

Often, the friction level depended on whom exactly Veeam had approached in a given company. The tendency was to market to the highest-ranking technology person at the firm, usually the CTO. But their core customer was really a hands-on IT professional, almost certainly not the CTO.

Seeing their customers in this way flew in the face of conventional marketing wisdom, which encourages us to separate our customers by strata. It's easy to be fooled by looking purely at market segments, and this results in missed opportunities. Veeam ended up realizing, "Our core customer is actually found all the way up and down this diagram, in all sizes of company, not just one." Some of Ratmir's executives were skeptical, but this way of organizing their successes and failures brought about useful discussion. It was provocative and made people think.

They realized that their core customer was not the person who made the financial decision to buy their products. It was the person who actually *used* the products, whose career depended on the company's backup software working well so that they could sleep peacefully at night. That person would then make a compelling case to whoever made the financial decision.

So, having defined their core customer, Veeam could focus on them more exclusively. They continued developing products for IT professionals, aiming to sell to and serve this cohort in all segments.

The key learnings were twofold:

1. Veeam needed to build products for their core customers and avoid getting distracted when other customers asked for new features. Their core customers would validate which features were really needed. Ratmir couldn't ignore the others and needed to answer their questions, but he wasn't building products for them. When a noncore customer asked for more features, that created more complexity and points of potential failure.

2. Veeam's core customers were found in every single market segment. Approaching the wrong person generally didn't yield a sale, but marketing to the right person was much more successful.

This core customer definition helped to focus their strategy for the next eight years as they built the business to over one billion in revenues.

HOW TO WRITE YOUR CORE CUSTOMER DEFINITION

The core customer definition should describe a real person with real needs. Veeam followed a process over multiple facilitated sessions that included the following steps:

1. Make a short list of the customers you love to serve (not necessarily your largest customers) and discuss:
    □ Who is the primary user of your product or service?
    □ What do they value about your product or service?

      □ What are their dreams and desires?

      □ What do they truly need?

      □ How might you uniquely offer what they truly need?

2. Make a short list of the customers that are the most challenging to serve and discuss:

      □ Why is it challenging to give them what they need?

      □ Learn about the characteristics of customers that you do not serve well, and consider avoiding these characteristics in your core customer definition.

3. Discuss, debate, and decide on the following:

      □ Who is our primary user?

      □ What do they really need?

      □ What do we provide that is unique to us that solves this need?

4. Develop your core customer definition, and limit it to twenty-five words or less:

      □ Avoid corporate jargon. Use simple words.

      □ Remove any "fluff" (marketing words).

      □ Use language that conveys feelings and experiences.

Focus on the Core Customer's Greatest Need (BioPlus)

BioPlus is a national specialty pharmacy that deals in medications for serious and life-threatening conditions, such as cancer, arthritis, and immune system disorders. They pride themselves on becoming very involved with each patient's situation, ensuring that medication regimens are followed exactly. The company had reached $126 million in revenues when their CEO, Dr. Stephen Vogt, invited me to join him on their journey in 2012. We have served Dr. Vogt and BioPlus for more than a decade.

Back in 2012, BioPlus was working with four key groups of stakeholders. They were (1) doctors who prescribe medications, (2) patients who use them, (3) insurance companies who pay for them, and (4) pharmaceutical suppliers who create them. When we started to explore the question of who BioPlus' core customer might be, Dr. Vogt and his team thought it was either the insurance companies who paid or the doctors who referred and prescribed the therapies. I had to ask, "But, what about the patients who actually take your medicines?" Dr. Vogt and his team needed to be more intentional about this defini-tion, and posing these questions really made them think.

YOUR CORE CUSTOMER IS THE PRIMARY PERSON WHO USES YOUR PRODUCT AND SERVICES. THIS IS THE PERSON YOU NEED TO DEFINE THE PRODUCT FOR AND COMPLETELY SATISFY AND DELIGHT.

Your core customer is the primary person who uses your product and services. This is the person you need to define the product for and completely satisfy and delight.

Through our discussions, the BioPlus team came to understand that their core customer was actually the patient. The other stake-holders—the doctors who prescribed the drugs and the insurance company that paid for them—were important, but they were not the ones who would be using the product. "It's the patient," Dr. Vogt said, experiencing something of an epiphany. "The patient is the one who is sick and who needs the treatment. It's for the patient that we have to create a fantastic customer experience." Up until then, he'd been focusing on the other groups. This shift would have huge implications.

"But they don't sign off on the drug or recommend it," the team discussed, "or even know the first thing about it." They do, however, experience every aspect of consuming the medication—the full life cycle of the process—and they respond dynamically to every other part of the chain. It's not about who pays for the product or service but who uses it that defines the core customer. Since the patient actually uses the medicines, in this case, the patient is the core customer. The other three groups of stakeholders are also important; they are secondary customers who also need to be serviced and satisfied.

This realization spurred a discussion about what the patient really needed. The BioPlus team discussed "what the customer really hated but had to put up with."[1]

They identified the patients' greatest pain. They had to wait about eighty-four business hours—more than ten business days—to receive approval once the medicine was prescribed. This is due to the fact that BioPlus' patients suffer from life-threatening diseases that require very expensive treatments. I think we can all agree that when someone is suffering from a life-threatening disease, waiting more than two weeks to get approval for medicine is painful and unacceptable. Yet, these patients had to live with this delay right after being given a terrifying diagnosis.

---

1   Patrick Thean, *Rhythm: How to Achieve Breakthrough Execution and Accelerate Growth,* (Austin, TX: Greenleaf Book Group Press, 2014).

The BioPlus team had an epiphany: How could they allow their core customer to suffer in this way? They had to focus and find a way to significantly reduce this wait time!

Dr. Vogt called me, anxious and excited, to announce that his team had decided this delay was unacceptable. "What they really need," he told me, "is to have approval within two hours." If they were somehow able to get the wait down to two hours, they would be forty times faster than all their competition. They would change their industry and change the lives of their patients at the same time!

They decided to go all in on this industry-leading promise and built a process to solve the problem. Each patient would necessarily have a completely different experience, but each one would receive the same promise: approval in two hours. As soon as a prescription was requested, a BioPlus representative would get on the phone with the patient's insurer and work to get the approval. Nobody else in the industry was emphasizing this niche understanding of the patients' needs in the same way.

I congratulated Dr. Vogt on this bold shift and asked how he felt about it. "Frankly, I was thinking that eight hours or one day would already be an amazing outcome. One day would be ten times better than our competition. But the team insisted that the patient, who is suffering, should not have to wait a whole day, or even eight hours, to get an answer. Two hours is a very ambitious goal," he said. "It might not even be reachable. But I don't want to smother my team's enthusiasm. I think, if they're prepared to put in the work to get the delay down to two hours, they'll figure out a way." And thus, the "Two-Hour Patient Acceptance Guarantee" was born.

What happened next was a complete reworking of their internal systems and the approval process. They achieved this remarkable feat, promising approval not twice as fast as their competition, or ten times, but forty times faster! This advantage carried them from revenues of $176 million to over $800 million in a little more than three years. In 2023, BioPlus was purchased by Elevance, part of the Nautic Partners portfolio of companies, for a large, undisclosed sum. The new owners had commissioned McKinsey Consulting to research and find the best specialty pharmacy in the country. McKinsey's answer was BioPlus.

Now, if they'd decided that their core customer were the doctors, they wouldn't have needed to do any of this. They'd have spent time on designing the doctor-patient portal to make life easier for the physician but not necessarily the patient. And if the insurance company were their core customer, they'd stretch the process out, not optimize it. After all, insurers want you to get pissed off and find another way! None of those things would have created the remarkable revenues that BioPlus achieved. Instead, they worked to understand the core customer's pain and focused on relieving it.

Dr. Vogt and his team at BioPlus changed their industry forever and significantly improved the lives of their patients. Over the years, his competition has had to play catch up and also improve their processes to reduce approval time. Because of Dr. Vogt's leadership, all patients who suffer these life-threatening diseases today benefit from reduced wait times for approval.

BioPlus demonstrated the power of determining the identity of your core customer, focusing on them, and then eliminating from their experience something they hate. It has proved to be a stunningly successful move, the kind that can happen when you intentionally build your client's journey around your core customer. BioPlus' journey continues, as they have posted a spectacular 968 percent growth over the last ten years.

FOCUS ON THE CORE CUSTOMER'S JOURNEY

These case studies demonstrate the power and success that come from deciding to build products, services, and even a customer journey that is completely dedicated to core customers.

I asked Michael to share his experience about core customers.

MICHAEL'S PERSPECTIVE

Every company ends up going through some pivots before they get where they need to be. Each of these could be a catalyst for innovation, and it's the right customer input that typically steers us in the right direction. If we are creating solutions in a vacuum, we'll miss the customer. Instead, we need to incorporate customer feedback and take an iterative approach.

From our early days at AvidXchange, we have always been obsessed with understanding our core customer's needs and designing the best customer journey possible. During our early days, we had a product called AvidBid, which was a reverse auction platform for bid management. Our customers were using AvidBid maybe once or twice a quarter for strategic sourcing events. They were telling us, "We're not sure how valuable this is. We don't use it very often." But they also said, "When we're sourcing these contracts, it generates a lot of paper invoices, and that's a problem. Maybe you could help us with that?" My initial natural reaction was, "Well, that's not what we do, we're a bid management company." But over the next year and a half, we found that this feedback highlighted a much bigger problem our customers had: managing their accounts payable and their invoice processing. What they really meant was that while AvidBid was interesting and provided some value, it was not as valuable as we would have liked to believe. It was not useful to them on a daily basis. By paying close attention to their experience and needs, we overcame our own bias and realized that helping them deal with accounts payable on a daily basis would be much more valuable to them.

So we strained our ears, listened, and pivoted toward working on a product that would help with accounts payable. Our core customer told us what was valuable to them, but it was hard to hear at first, because we loved our own products. However, our obsession over the customers' needs soon helped us pivot away from AvidBid toward something much more worthwhile to our customers.

Then around 2010, we started to hear another request at our user conference. Our core customers shared that they were still paying paper invoices with paper checks but preferred to pay electronically. And again, we found ourselves replying, "We're not really in that business. Talk to your banks or your accounts people. Maybe they can solve it." But the request didn't go away, so in 2011, I brought thirty customers to Charlotte and asked them, "What problem do you want us to solve?"

One customer stood up, representing a big West Coast real estate firm, and he said, "I've got three hundred assets spread across the country and lots of accounts with twenty-six different banks. Because of acquisitions, we've got seven different accounting systems. It's driving me nuts. I want to run a single payment process for the whole company." Others in the room recognized that they had the same problem. And once they explained it, light bulbs went off.

No bank could solve this, and neither could their accounting systems. Thus, we created the AvidPay Network and used automation software we'd written back in 2002. Once it was in place, we grew at 30 percent for ten years in a row. That allowed us to become the business we are today and to execute our IPO in October 2021.

The key lesson is to figure out who your core customers are and listen to them. Let them help you by sharing their pains and needs. This allows you to build products that are confirmed solutions to customers' needs! Technology companies are famous for building products first and then looking for ways to use them. That's building a solution and then looking for a problem to solve. Instead, if you can control your own biases, strain your ears, and listen to your core customers, you might discover the right problem to solve before you spend a dime on building the solution.

The hard part was letting go of our own misconceptions and really listening to the right customers: our core customers. By doing that, we got to the heart of what we needed to solve. Our core customers helped us understand the size and shape of the real problem. If your core customers see enough value, they might even be willing to share in the cost of developing the product.

Build products that your core customers need to use. It's the simplest concept, but it's hard to implement. It is tempting to build products that you think people want. It's nice to think that you have all the answers, but in reality, you don't! There is no success in building products that your core customers do not value and will not buy. It is OK to lead with innovation, but do not forget to ask your core customers what they need; otherwise, your product will be a solution looking for a problem. Instead, clearly identify what problems your core customers need solved, and go solve those problems.

IT IS OK TO LEAD WITH INNOVATION, BUT DO NOT FORGET TO ASK YOUR CORE CUSTOMERS WHAT THEY NEED; OTHERWISE, YOUR PRODUCT WILL BE A SOLUTION LOOKING FOR A PROBLEM. INSTEAD, CLEARLY IDENTIFY WHAT PROBLEMS YOUR CORE CUSTOMERS NEED SOLVED, AND GO SOLVE THOSE PROBLEMS.

Focus By Saying YES to Core Customers, NO to Everyone Else

Focus actually means saying NO much more often than saying YES. Not all your customers are core customers. I have yet to meet a company that has that perfect scenario. All successful companies receive product requests and new ideas from customers. We usually have more opportunities than we have resources to chase them. How do you decide what to say YES to versus NO?

Remember, every time you say YES to something, you are saying NO to many other things because of your limited resources. Be careful to clearly segment your customer base. Know who your core customers are and who they are not. Not all customers are equal. Do not use your precious resources to build anything that your core customers do not need.

Mort O'Sullivan shared his strategy when we discussed how his cash automation company, ARCA, meets its core customers' needs. "Our competitors are bigger than us," he explained, "and can be arrogant and difficult to work with. They would tell their customers what they needed—how many machines and what kind—rather than working with them to understand their needs. We recognized that our customers didn't like that, so we took a different approach that was collaborative, consultative, and more flexible. We asked for their advice and listened."

Mort put in place a system for assessing those needs. "We made lots of site visits and really engaged with the customers. Our sales team worked to understand what our customers were looking for and what problems they needed to solve. Then, a separate consulting team would spend up to two days with the customer doing deep analysis of their cash volumes, doing time-and-motion studies, and then feeding that data back to us. After we'd closed the sale, our after-sales team visited and made sure the machines had 100 percent uptime and tracked any new needs. It was all hand in hand. I honestly believe that's been a simple but decisive difference."

The process of listening to your core customers helps you to intentionally develop products with them squarely in mind. Some firms harness the power of their core customers by creating customer advisory boards, as Michael Praeger did, to turn their knowledge into product decisions. It's important that advisory boards are chosen from within your core customer group.

Don't fall into the trap of assuming that your biggest customer is your core customer. Biggest does not mean most profitable or most easily served. If your biggest customers are not your core customers, you will experience a lot of friction and stress in delivering your products and services. Remember that your core customers enjoy working with your teams and vice versa because of the strong fit of your products to their needs.

Focus your strategy on your core customer. Build what they need, and then say NO to everyone else.

BOTTOM LINE

1. Your core customer is a real person, not a market segment.
2. Your core customer is someone who is a great fit for your products and services. You enjoy serving them today, and they have the ability to grow with you into your future.
3. Take the time to define your core customer. Be prepared for vigorous discussion with competing points of view.
4. Achieve complete alignment throughout your company on who your core customer is.
5. Build your products and services for this core customer. Other customers may also buy and use what you offer, even though it was designed and customized for your core customer.
6. Your core customer might exist in multiple market segments.
7. Focus your strategy by saying "Yes" to building things that your core customers need. Then say "No" to others, especially when their requests might conflict with the needs of your core customers.
8. Focus on making your core customer happy instead of trying to make all of your customers happy. If you are prioritizing for everyone, you are prioritizing for no one.
9. Consider what your core customers hate putting up with. There might be a winning move waiting there for you.
10. Invest in understanding your core customer's needs through visits and research. Put yourself in their shoes in order to learn and empathize with their experience of interacting with you.

CHAPTER 12

OUR JOURNEY CONTINUES

"The journey of a thousand miles must begin with a single step."

–LAO TZE

Many founders dream of taking their company from startup to IPO as a step toward building a great business that endures as a legacy beyond themselves. These seven practices have helped Michael and many other CEOs and senior leaders achieve success in leading their companies and teams.

On October 13, 2021, AvidXchange successfully completed their IPO. They currently trade on NASDAQ under the symbol AVDX. This is an incredible accomplishment as less than one percent of all startups go on to achieve an IPO. Only a fraction of those that make it remain led by founder CEOs.

MICHAEL'S PERSPECTIVE

AvidXchange's journey to becoming a public company was actually a twenty-three-year process of building the business one customer and one vertical industry segment at a time. Great companies are not built overnight; they are a result of many critical decisions made at momentous stages of growth by the founder and key leaders.

At the end of the day, in order to be successful, you really only need to get critical decisions correct in the following five areas:

- Your talent and recruiting the right leaders for the right level of scale
- Your growth strategies and business model
- Your execution and operational scale strategies that drive your profitability and margin profile
- Your financial and cash management strategies that create the "oxygen" needed to both survive and thrive
- Lastly, the culture of your business, which is the combination of mindsets and behaviors that define what makes your culture unique

Being a founding leader of a high-growth business is not for the faint of heart, as the day-to-day decisions can be overwhelming at times. Use the seven practices to prioritize your time and energy toward making the best decisions possible in these five areas. You will be able to bring a new level of clarity and purpose to your organization, which will enable your team to thrive and deliver strong performance results.

The last nugget of wisdom that I continuously share with other entrepreneurs is to surround yourself with the best advisors, board members, and coaches possible so that you can continue growing and developing your own leadership capabilities and keep up with the growth of your business.

As we celebrated AvidXchange's IPO and hugged, Michael said, "Buddy, we did it!"

I corrected him. "No, Michael. *You* did it!"

The thought briefly flashed through my mind: I wonder if Michael still needs a coach like me for the next stage of his journey.

He must have read my mind, because he flashed a huge grin. "Buddy, you'd better gear up for the next leg of our journey. We are going to build a billion-dollar company!"

TO LEARN MORE ABOUT OUR JOURNEY AND TOOLS AND TO STAY CONNECTED WITH PATRICK, PLEASE VISIT PATRICKTHEAN.COM.

PATRICK THEAN

Patrick is a best-selling author, speaker, and serial entrepreneur. In 1996, Patrick was honored as EY Entrepreneur of the Year for propelling his venture to #151 on the Inc. 500 (now the Inc. 5000).

With his first book, *Rhythm: How to Achieve Breakthrough Execution and Accelerate Growth,* Thean shares a simple system for encouraging teams to execute better and faster. He reveals early signs of common setbacks in entrepreneurship and how to make the necessary adjustments. His tools were integrated into the EO/MIT Entrepreneurial Masters Programme where Patrick served as Program Co-Chair for seven years. CEOs using his method have achieved increased company valuation by 10X, and have achieved Unicorn status and a successful IPO on Nasdaq.

Happily married for over thirty years, he enjoys spending time with his wife and two daughters as their family pursues their dreams. Patrick is passionate about Samaritan's Feet, an organization that serves children by providing shoes and preventing life-threatening foot-borne diseases. He helped the organization execute their first BHAG of putting ten million pairs of shoes on the feet of children around the world.

Currently the CEO and Co-Founder of Rhythm Systems, he is helping CEOs experience breakthroughs to achieve their dreams and goals.

MICHAEL PRAEGER

Michael is the Co-Founder, Chairman, and CEO of AvidXchange (Nasdaq listed—AVDX), the leading provider of accounts payable and payment automation solutions for middle market companies. Since founding AvidXchange more than 20 years ago, Michael has led the company to more than 8,000 customers and over 1.2 million suppliers with over 1,700 team members nationwide.

An expert on fintech, payments innovation, entrepreneurism, and leadership, Michael has been an active participant and speaker at various industry conferences, as well as a Forbes contributor with appearances in *Authority Magazine, Business Insider, Inc.*, and *The Wall Street Journal*. Michael was also named the 2018 Business Person of the Year by the *Charlotte Business Journal* as well as the 2022 EY Entrepreneur of the Year Southeast Winner. Michael is also the 2022 Inductee for the Carolina Entrepreneur Hall of Fame.

Before establishing AvidXchange, Michael was Co-Founder of PlanetResume.com, a technology career enhancement and recruiting site that successfully completed its merger with CareerShop.com in November 1999. Prior to that, he was Co-Founder and CEO of InfoLink Partners, a software company specializing in automating the tax billing and collection functions for municipalities.

Michael received a BSBA in Finance from Georgetown University. Michael resides in Charlotte, North Carolina, on Lake Norman.

ABOUT RHYTHM SYSTEMS, INC.

We are dedicated to helping CEOs and leaders succeed and achieve their dreams. We have lived this purpose for over two decades and have continuously refined our time-tested methodology and systems. Our proven track record is demonstrated by the 62% of our business which comes from customer referrals.

Rhythm Systems offers a solution that is tailor-made for mid-market, growing companies:

- THINK PLAN DO®: A proven method to develop and execute Winning Move strategies
- AI-powered software that keeps your teams focused, aligned, and accountable to achieving their best results
- Consulting and coaching to help you develop winning strategies and execute them across the entire organization

CEOs and leaders who have engaged with us have achieved amazing results:

- 10X growth in revenues, profits, and company valuation
- IPO with continued success quarter after quarter as a public company

- Growing even while their industry shrinks by taking market share from their competition

Your journey and experience matter. Your company matters. You matter. Working with us, you will experience:

- A more joyous path as you succeed and build stronger relationships with your team
- Strong focus on an inspiring future that helps you communicate your vision and Winning Move strategies so that everyone knows how they make a difference in the company
- Winning habits and practices that cascade goals, resulting in successful execution in teams throughout your company

Scan the QR Code to learn more or visit:
www.CEO7Practices.com/book/RS

STRATEGY EXECUTION CONSULTING

Rhythm Systems' consultants are strategy execution experts. Each advisor is a highly seasoned professional with deep experience in a range of disciplines and industries. Most are former clients, CEOs, and executive leaders who have experienced the challenges of running organizations firsthand. They have used Rhythm to grow their own companies and are passionate about helping CEOs and leaders achieve great success.

FOR CEOS AND EXECUTIVE LEADERS:

- **Strategy Execution Planning Sessions:** Every consultant is a master facilitator and expert in using Rhythm's methodology, processes, and tools to lead teams in the development of strategy and execution, focused annual plans, and actionable quarterly plans. Rhythm Systems experts are highly skilled at drawing out and uncovering innovative solutions that may have been previously overlooked.
- **CEO and Executive Coaching Programs:** Coaching that guides CEOs and executives away from pitfalls and helps

them apply the seven practices contained in this book. These are uncommon learnings that have helped countless executives navigate business challenges, communicate well with all stakeholders, and achieve their desired results. Rhythm Systems coaches will help you uncover potential blind spots, lead with intention, and surpass your personal and business goals.

FOR CONSULTANTS:

- **The Rhythm Coaching Network:** If you are interested in developing your coaching, facilitation, and consulting skills to help CEOs succeed, we encourage you to explore the Rhythm Coaching Network. Find out how to leverage our training, software, and methodology to develop and grow your own successful consulting business.

Scan the QR Code to learn more or visit:

www.CEO7Practices.com/book/consulting

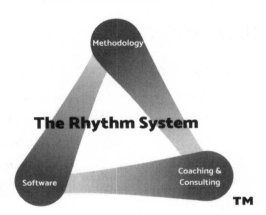

INDEX

A

abdication 103–104

accountability 15, 23, 116, 137, 152

alignment 27, 99–116, 152

Ankrum, Amy 74, 78

annual planning

A-Player 160–166

ARCA 175, 176, 204

AVDX 14, 207, 219

AvidInvoice

AvidPay Network 202

AvidXchange 14, 16, 17, 42–45, 48, 55–58, 69, 91, 94, 105, 106, 124–127, 130, 133, 134, 143, 144, 153, 159, 171, 174, 177, 178, 191, 201, 207–209

B

behavior 38, 122, 124–130, 135–136, 139–140, 143–144, 163

binary thinking 44

BioPlus 49, 50, 191, 196–200

blind spot 67, 73–76